"I had to read the book a second time; it was so good. I laughed and cried throughout."
— **Doris Swenson**

"The book made me think of things I hadn't thought about for years, and other things I had never thought about before."
— **Dr. Terry Tuchin**

"When I read this book, it gave me a feeling of hope for the future."
— **Joeen Ciannella**

"The book is thoughtful, whimsical and profound...gives us hope as we consider our human journey. ...helps us use our histories to find our way into the present.

Monotheism, called by different names is shared by Jews, Christians and Muslims. From atheists to believer's the author's love of ideas and learning urges us to gain new insights and harmony into our lives. This book pays homage to the known and the unknown."

— **Cipora O. Schwartz**

WALKING ALL OVER GOD'S HEAVEN

BY RICHARD ROUKEMA

IPG

WALKING ALL OVER GOD'S HEAVEN

Published by:
Intermedia Publishing Group, Inc.
P.O. Box 2825
Peoria, Arizona 85380
www.intermediapub.com

ISBN 978-1-935529-79-8

All Scripture quotations are taken from the King James Version of the Holy Bible unless indicated otherwise.

DEDICATION

To my parents
Meindert and Grace Roukema
With love and gratitude

FOREWORD

People usually want their world to make sense. It is certainly easier when there is a logical progression; then, upon reaching the desired outcome, there are no surprises. There are also surprises we welcome, because they are sources of pleasure and represent some of the more joyful aspects of our life experience. If someone made a reference to candy coated popcorn treats with a prize inside every box, you would think of "Cracker Jack" and you might remember the anticipation with which you searched for your surprise in the box.

When you hear someone has written a book about heaven, you most likely assume the author is a theologian or spiritual leader of sorts; you are probably not thinking of a psychiatrist, but Dr. Richard (Dick) Roukema, is not an ordinary psychiatrist. In getting to know his history and hearing him describe his life, it starts sounding more like a spiritual pilgrimage, rather than a journey focused exclusively on medicine, science, and the practice of psychiatry. Dick is not unlike the reference to "Cracker Jack" with the prize inside the box. He is unassuming, quiet, humble, and yet the warmth and gentleness that emanates from within him is like an unexpected gift. Dick Roukema continues to bring joy to my life, and to every life touched by the gift of his presence in the world.

My relationship with Dick came to life during my tenure at Christian Health Care Center (CHCC) in Wyckoff, NJ. Already a catalyst for change, Dick helped CHCC become a facility known for providing a "continuum of care" for people at various stages in life, as well as for those persons living with diverse expressions of psychological and emotional problems for which they could receive support and treatment.

At CHCC, I was charged with the task of serving the community as "Coordinator of Church Relations." Dr. Roukema, at that point working as consultant in the Department of Pastoral Care, became my mentor. A relationship which initially appeared to be an odd match-up became a rich experience and a blessing to my life. What I did not know about Dick is that from the early years of his life, growing up with a foundation based on Dutch Reformed theology, the seeds of his own spiritual life were planted. In fact, upon finishing high school, he was voted most likely to become a minister. Although he speaks with much gratitude about his vocation as a psychiatrist, it takes only one meeting with Dick to realize that, regardless of job title, this is a man with the heart of a pastor.

Growing out of a sensitive and compassionate appreciation for clergy, there were many occasions, during his years in private practice, when he was able to work directly with clergy. When I came on staff, he was asked to work with me regarding strategies that would offer ongoing support to clergy and the congregations they were called to serve. It is through his efforts on their behalf that Dick created, developed and fostered opportunities to nurture them in their ministry, as well as support them in their own spiritual awakening both in terms of their personal and professional development.

Over the years, Dick heard the cry of those shepherding congregations. He became increasingly aware of the ever growing demands and expectations faced by clergy, as well as the stress and strain under which they were trying to cope. It was clear that, in their ministry setting, clergy, regardless of their tradition, felt ill equipped to respond to the often present psychological and emotional issues of the people under their care. In the spirit of a shepherd caring for his sheep, Dick authored two books, one entitled *Shepherding the Shepherd*, addressing the unique needs of clergy, and *Counseling for the Soul in Distress*, which is more like a reference manual for clergy in order to give them tools for understanding and responding to the many emotional and psychological issues presented to them in their ministry.

In *Walking All over God's Heaven*, the reader will experience a refreshing look at many of the unanswered questions in life. Sometimes we fear the unanswered questions. We believe they will weaken our faith, when, in fact, the experience of stretching the familiar limits of our faith can strengthen and deepen it. This realization affirms that even without answers, God is present with us, even as we wrestle with the questions that so occupy our existence.

This book invites the reader to join the author on a journey, which takes the form of a dream. In the story of the dream we see, in him, the heart of a soul longing for God. As the story begins, Dick reaches the end of his long life, and after arriving in heaven, he first experiences "a sense of uncertainty and mystery." It seems unclear to him whether he is there to stay or only visiting. In either case, it becomes a chance for him to satisfy his curiosity about life on the "other side."

In the initial phase of his heavenly journey, the author takes us on a trip throughout the celestial realm where he encounters a number of groups. It is expected that everyone will join a group, each of which is dedicated to a particular theme which reflects interests similar to those areas which became the point of focus while on earth. The groups are broken into categories, for example: a group made up of biblical prophets, another for the elite, and another for doubters. There is even a group for doctors and one for lawyers, as well as disciples and saints.

The author's dream became the metaphor for his own spiritual awakening and a platform for reflecting on many of the questions we wrestle with in life. These include questions that range from who gains access to heaven, to the question of why there is evil, as well as how God actually works in the world. Dick gives himself permission to consider and wrestle with topics which are complex and often controversial.

In visiting the various groups, he sees the vast number of heavenly residents, who like the author himself, are not only debating over the most heated controversial issues, but are discovering they have not resolved or been able to let go of the things that defined their earthly existence. So the struggle continues, even in heaven. You can see the unfolding of his life journey as Dick looks squarely in the face of the discomfort and uncertainty that is experienced as one grows increasingly aware of the complexity of the world and the concerns of humanity which reveal a profound level of vulnerability.

In thoughtful and playfully provocative ways, questions which can usually leave people a little squeamish, become food for thought and the deepening of ones resolve to believe that God, in whose heaven he takes this journey, joins us in our confusion and search for understanding.

The message of *Walking All over God's Heaven* speaks to anyone who finds themselves with more questions than answers. But it is also for people whose life is defined by some expression of faith. It is a book that challenges readers to open themselves up to questions and concerns not covered by traditional orthodoxy and biblical revelation. Yet, in a way which celebrates his own Christian faith, Dick affirms a timeless truth, consistent with the tenets of traditional orthodoxy, which is that, apart from clear answers, there is hope.

I would imagine some would underestimate the value of such a book. Along with wanting life to make sense, many people look for ways to avoid the tough questions and controversial topics that, despite our best efforts keep coming up in our minds and daily lives. In *Walking All over God's Heaven*, Dr.

Roukema courageously identifies many of these contemporary topics and invites his readers to be just as brave in pondering questions which for them are still unanswered. I dare say if there are those who are tempted to dismiss his courage as heresy, I would imagine that springs from the fear of wrestling with God. When we get honest with ourselves we can be faced with the discomfort of acknowledging our human frailties, which may lead us to close our minds and hearts. As the story unfolds, it is clear that there is value in asking tough questions and naming difficult issues, even when the answers remain well out of sight.

In his role as a psychiatrist, he spent nearly half of his life in the field of medicine and psychiatry. His work has gone well beyond the realm of the typical psychiatrist in private practice. He has spearheaded programs and held positions in medicine and psychiatry which have helped to elevate the attention given to issues of mental health as a vehicle which can promote healing within the whole person.

The author's passion for people, generated by a longing for God, makes *Walking All over God's Heaven* a must-read for anyone wrestling with many of the unanswered and unspoken questions about life, which Dick approaches thoughtfully, thoroughly, and carefully.

Walking All over God's Heaven also invites the reader to go to a place of thoughtful reflection. It reminds us that God does not sit back, uninvolved. God is not distancing himself from the cries of humanity, but comes alongside weeping with us in our pain, suffering with us in times of sorrow, and sharing the ache of our hearts troubled and burdened by life. It also brings a message which plants seeds of hope through others, who become the tangible expressions of divine love. It is this hope, an often unexpressed longing, which, on the one hand, may be found in heaven, and yet, on the other, may also be an anchor that helps us to hold on in this life. Maybe it is in the ways we are connected to one another, and the ways we experience the celebration of human diversity, that help us learn the importance of holding onto each other.

When thinking about this life or the next, one is left with more uncertainty than clarity. Never is there a promise in Scripture that we can or will ever understand all there is to know about the nature and character of God. Yet, it does not mean we need to pretend the questions do not exist. In *Walking All over God's Heaven* you can join Dr. Roukema in quiet contemplation of these questions as you enjoy his imagined and uniquely refreshing view of heaven.

Dr. Michael Avila, Executive Director
Sojourners Family Resource Center
Hasbrouck Heights, New Jersey

Acknowledgements

Many thanks to my friends and colleagues who made suggestions for the writing of this book. They encouraged me to complete the work and showed a genuine interest in the portrayal of heaven.

Clergymen who were kind enough to help me and make suggestions include the Reverends James Knol, Michael Avila, William Falkner, Timothy Dunn and my pastor, Nolan Polsma.

I cannot forget my fellow tennis players; Dave Shaw, Joe Clark, Paul O'Leary and my good friends; Doris Swenson, Donna and Bill Jacoby, Cipora Schwartz and Joeen Cianella. Family members who saw earlier versions of the manuscript include Jim and Meg Kuhn, Susan and Greg Roukema, Harriet and Marvin Abma, Grace Deboer and Dan Minkema. My friends and colleagues Drs. Alba and Raul Ludmer and Terry Tuchin gave me unusual encouragement.

I owe a deep level of gratitude to my friend and mentor Richard Paris, who critiqued the manuscript many times. I appreciate his patience and the gift of his valuable time.

And finally, many thanks to Terry Whalin for his excellent guidance, JoHanna Gratz for her fine editing and Floyd Orfield for the pleasing cover design.

PROLOGUE

Most Christians believe in a spiritual life in heaven after their earthly life is complete. Life in the great beyond is usually portrayed as eternal peace, tranquility and singing praise to God. However, few writers have described the possibilities of life in heaven.

The New Testament reveals little of the actual conditions there, and what the inhabitants will be doing. We are given some specifics – no crying, death, sorrow or pain. There is no marriage, and Christ spoke of "many mansions." In the book of Revelation, St. John gives us a vision of heaven with the judgment of God for all our earthly deeds. Much of this last chapter of the Bible consists of vivid pictures of struggles on Earth and victories in heaven, but little of life in heaven for the average inhabitant.

St. Augustine speculated about heaven in his book *The City of God.* He said that all heaven's citizens would have the same beautiful body and be thirty years old, about the same age as Jesus was at the time He began His ministry. Infants, he explained, would be adults in heaven and through regeneration be set free from original sin. He goes on to say that when St. Paul writes in 1 Corinthians 13 that "we see through a glass darkly," meaning that we will not see the actual face of God but instead see Him as a Spirit. St. Augustine says that the saints will be able to see God whether their eyes are open or closed.

In spite of his extensive writings in the *Divine Comedy*, Dante does not give many clues as to how life will be lived in heaven. He is more concerned about where various souls will go. For example, those guilty of fraud – which Dante says God hates the most – like fakers, robbers, hypocrites, and simoniacs (those that sell favors) will be punished. Dante lists three hierarchies and different levels of heaven, related to rewards for earthly lives well-lived. Those in higher realms will enjoy God more, although all in heaven will be content. The highest level consists of souls, who will live the contemplative life, such as Mary, Gabriel, St. Paul, St. James and others. But with all Dante's pictures of life in heaven, he gives little imagination to what the general inhabitants will be doing.

Another writer who has ventured into the possible way we might live in heaven is the philosopher, writer and Christian apologist C.S. Lewis. In *The Great Divorce*, Lewis takes a bus ride to heaven in what is later revealed as a dream. He says that in heaven, a person has no needs and can get anything one wants by just imagining it. Can I be useful in heaven? Lewis says that one's talents and abilities learned on Earth are not needed in heaven. He dreams of ghosts in hell trying to get those in heaven to come to hell. Lewis is careful to acknowledge that he has no special information about heaven. One of his characters says,

"Give no poor fool the pretext to think ye are claiming knowledge of what no mortal knows." Furthermore, in the preface to the book, he makes it clear that what he writes is a fantasy, and that he has no wish to have the reader regard the contents as factual.

In a recent novel, *The Five People You Meet in Heaven,* written by Mitch Albom, the author explores what happens to an elderly man when he dies suddenly. He does not find heaven to be a paradise, but rather a place where life on Earth makes sense as described by five people he knew on Earth, whom he meets in the hereafter. Eddie, the main character, discovers that what he did on Earth to help people was the purpose for which he lived. But little is said about what daily life is like in heaven.

My early years in elementary and high school were filled with religious training in a Protestant Christian school. Much later, as a psychiatrist, I worked extensively with clergy in consultation, or occasionally when they personally needed care. As I grew older, I was filled with wonder as to what the future might hold in the hereafter. Christians speak of the hope of reaching heaven. As a Christian, I share that hope. But what will it be like?

I want to make clear what I tried to portray in this book. Some of what I have written is memoir, as best as I can recall it. The rest is pure fantasy, imagery, a wish – yes, a visual picture of heaven's nature. None of what I have written should be thought of as a statement of theological doctrine or a treatise on eschatological truth.

It is my hope that the picture I paint of activities in heaven will be taken as a portrait for contemplation, a vehicle for the imagination and a template for discussion by interested groups.

Richard Roukema

**"There lives more faith in honest doubt,
Believe me, than in half the creeds."**

In Memoriam, Alfred Lord Tennyson

CHAPTER 1

The old spiritual says, "I'm going to walk all over God's Heaven ..." But what will that heaven be like?

If you believe in life after death and want to spend eternity there, just what will you do with all that time? Who will be there? Will it include all humans or just a select few? I can readily expect my friends to be there, but what about those difficult and disagreeable characters I met in this world? Will they be there too?

Will I be in a physical body or in a spiritual self or both? What will all those revered biblical prophets be doing, and how will the saints that followed be occupied? Will we see our family members who have predeceased us? Will it be all ease and singing in celestial choirs and relaxing on clouds? Wouldn't that be boring after awhile?

Perhaps we would be given a large dose of heavenly patience to handle all the inactivity? Or, by contrast, will there be work to do and plenty to keep us busy?

Heaven to me was always a vague, elusive, hard to conceive concept. From childhood, it was portrayed as a place where one lived a passive life, except for praising God and singing in the heavenly choir.

I have trouble associating that with some pleasures here on earth, where I am fully active. I think of the thrill of skiing down a snow-covered hill, swimming in a calm, blue lake, riding the breakers at the ocean or competing in a friendly tennis match.

I think of the joy of friendship with family and colleagues, the struggles of patient care, and successes with helping the mentally ill. I recall the challenges of intellectual pursuits in college and medical school, the variety of intimacies in family relationships; the satisfaction of various gastronomical, physical, and sexual appetites, the unheralded pleasures of reading a good novel or a well-documented book of non-fiction.

There must be something else going on in heaven. To the earthly mind, heaven sounds too simple, routine and – do I dare say it – boring. In suggesting this, I am aware of my ignorance of the true nature of heaven. It takes a certain amount of impertinence or even arrogance to imagine that our existence could be quite different in the after life than simply being content lying around on a cloud enjoying everlasting peace.

Admittedly, there are times in life, when living a peaceful life free of responsibilities, worries, emergencies or even the drudgery of everyday home and property maintenance sounds good to me. And let's not forget the constant getting and spending we do, by which, as Wordsworth suggests, "we lay waste our powers."

The other area that has always seemed curious to me is the unfinished lives most of us live. Could there be an opportunity in heaven to make right what we were not able to complete here on earth?

There certainly are some folks who seem to live truly fulfilled lives with a sense of completion. I am thinking of the laborer, who manages to raise a family and see his children complete college. He lives to see them move on to marriages and families of their own, and then lives out his own last years with a marriage still vital and intact.

Other examples are the professional persons who have lived their lives in relative fulfillment of their careers, having completed most of their goals in life, both professionally and personally. But many people, when they die, leave things undone, even if life isn't taken from them suddenly.

Is it possible that in heaven, we will have an opportunity to complete the work not finished here?

Could we finally speak the things we meant to say to the father we lost early, the mother who we never thanked enough for her tender care, or the spouse we failed to love and appreciate adequately? Will we be able to say things to our children which we had left unspoken? Will we be able to tell certain friends how much we appreciated their concern, just knowing that they were available when we needed them?

Will we be able to communicate with relatives we never saw – the grandparents whom we were too young to remember or who died in another country before we were born?

These were some of the thoughts that went through my mind from time to time as I grew older. Then one night I lay in bed thinking about the hike I had taken that day with friends and the casual lunch we had at a local restaurant. I felt relaxed and decided to read a bit before going to sleep. After a half hour of reading, as usually happens, I felt drowsy, turned off the light and promptly fell asleep.

Some time during the night, I had a dream that seemed at first to raise and then even answer some of my questions about heaven. It was a long dream, unlike the ordinary dreams I have had of present-day problems and interests or past issues that have lingered deep in the unconscious.

One of my recurring dreams since medical school involves taking a long examination and having trouble finishing on time. This is a replay of my second year in medical studies, when our pathology professor gave us detailed and exhausting three-hour essay exams. Ten percent of the class always failed to finish. How many times have I dreamed some version of that experience and then awakened, relieved that I had already passed the course and no longer had to suffer the anxiety and fear of failure?

This new, fresh and amazing dream came about without any warning. Although I have had difficulty remembering all of the details of the dream, I have recorded most of it here with perhaps a few details culled from my imagination, where memory failed.

Life had been good to me. God had blessed me and given me a long life by earthly standards. But in my dream, I suddenly arrived in heaven, sooner than I expected. I wasn't ready yet for this new adventure. I still felt there were a lot of things I had not finished here on earth, (not unlike my recurrent dream of the medical school exam). As many of my retired friends have said when asked if they are bored, "There's always more to do than I have time for."

Dreams often continue or try to work out the concerns of our daytime preoccupations. Parts of what we think about in our waking hours recur in our dreams. Sigmund Freud spoke of these bits as the "daytime residue." He maintained that dreams were wish fulfillments and therefore served a real purpose in maintaining our mental equilibrium. So it was not surprising that I should have a dream about the nature of heaven. The surprise, however, was the length of the dream and the detailed experiences I had throughout this journey.

In my dream I had lived a long life – into my nineties. But it was not clear whether I was just visiting heaven or whether I was a permanent resident. Had I died and arrived at heaven in this way or had I been given a temporary visa in some spiritual manner that only God could provide? My presence had a ring of uncertainty and mystery, like so much of the religious life. And as far as the dream was concerned it did not really matter, because what the dream told me about heaven was extraordinary.

What is heaven and what do the souls in heaven do with all their heavenly days? I had always been curious about the "other side." Here was my chance to find out, even though it was only in a dream. Just as I was so preoccupied with life in heaven, suddenly, in my dream, I was there.

I have read about near death experiences from which individuals had survived. To my surprise, in the dream I saw that bright light that many have reported. The light seemed to draw me away from my earthly existence. I remember nothing after that, until I arrived at the entrance to heaven.

Where were the famous pearly gates? Nowhere! Clouds? Yes. There was haze, fog and then a glorious sunshine, like I had never seen before. And there to welcome me along with a large group of other newcomers was – you guessed it – St. Peter. Yes, he was for real.

He was quite cordial and upbeat. He had a traditional white robe and sandals. His long flowing beard disguised his olive complexion. St. Peter was clearly in control of the situation, where his principle job was to welcome all newcomers to heaven. I later learned that he had some counseling roles as well. After some brief remarks, he referred me and others to his assistants, whose job was to orient us to heaven's wonders.

In my dream, I was pleasantly surprised that I had arrived in heaven. I have to admit that I wasn't always sure I would make it here. I have had my doubts about the whole business of heaven. It was always a hard place for me to imagine. The Bible speaks of many mansions, a home of leisure and peace, where we would have a spiritual existence and a perfect physical body, eternally praising God with the angels.

Yet few authors have written about the actual place or even fantasized about what heaven would really be like. Even theologians have been hesitant to venture comments about heavenly realms, except to speak in generalities, not daring to project their own thoughts on the subject.

As my doubt about heaven's existence has occasionally come to mind, I heard preachers say that to have doubts about one's faith is a good thing, that the measure of faith one has is related to awe, mystery and not understanding it all. And, knowing the workings of the human mind, I seriously wondered what we would do differently if we did know all the answers to existential questions.

Everything would be just a matter of fact. There would be no mystery about heaven, and faith would be unnecessary. Well, that's not the way God planned it. So, with me, faith won out, and I'm glad to say that I am here in heaven. At least one existential question is answered. There is a heaven, at least in my dream.

*****

Let me tell you about this amazing place. I hardly know where to begin. To my surprise, heaven is nothing like I had envisioned. Sometimes there are shades of gray, chiaroscuro like you would not believe. Suddenly, everything is white, followed instantly by colors you cannot imagine, better than any field of wildflowers or garden of tulips and daffodils or the best artist's rendition of a brilliant landscape. Then, just as abruptly, there are no colors at all.

The next thing I noticed was that it was hard to recognize anyone. I had real trouble placing in memory an old college friend. He would show up out of the blue or sometimes through a cloud, and then he would keep changing right before my eyes.

One minute he appeared with an earthly body. The next time, just as suddenly, he became invisible and was a spirit, but still able to communicate with me. Carrying on a conversation with someone you can't see at first is very disconcerting, but I quickly became accustomed to it. After a while, it didn't seem all that different from talking on an earthly telephone or communicating by e-mail.

Another weird phenomenon – right in the middle of a conversation with one of my old buddies about the nature of heaven, he might disappear, and another friend would take over. It's one thing to put up with people interrupting you, as I remember on Earth, but when they simply vanish and somebody else appears, it's very distracting.

But when I checked out this situation with an old resident here, he said,

"You get used to it after a while." In heaven, conditions seemed less predictable than they did before, at least when you first arrive here.

I noticed that folks from various countries were able to speak to each other without translators. They all spoke the same language. I can best describe what happens in heaven by telling you that each person here is able to talk using a heavenly Esperanto. That made it possible to communicate with anyone regardless of their earthly origin.

The other thing that was hard to figure out was my precarious balance. Was I standing on a cloud? Was it just air? It was hard to take a step. But as it turned out, concern about standing or walking was not necessary. One of the residents told me what to do. "All you have to do is think about being somewhere else, and you'll be there in a flash."

It reminded me of being in the fun house at an amusement park, walking on a moving platform or seeing the distortions of your image in mirrors. As with the fun house, heaven was one illusion after another. Yet, as I remained there, I began to acclimate to the environment. I will tell you about it as I go on.

We often picture the saints and the prophets of old among the clouds dressed in white robes, looking beatific, smiling benignly and, of course, singing continuous choruses of joy. But I didn't see much of that. A few of the old-timers were dressed in white, but those who appeared younger had a choice of types of clothes and colors.

Those who looked young wore drab outfits of grey and black, not unlike the present crowd of youngsters I remembered. The folks who appeared middle-aged wore the brightest outfits. Some preferred robes, some old English formal wear; others wore casual peasant clothes with bright, electric colors – red, yellow, orange, violet – reminiscent of some African tribal costumes or ancient Incan civilizations.

I was told that on any given day one could opt to wear as many different outfits as one could dream up. I noticed a few souls would choose many-colored coats that reminded me of the biblical Joseph, except that the colors were so brilliant, that only an earthly sunset could rival them.

All the choices of color, type of dress, modesty and flair – for some this was an unexpected bonus of being in heaven, especially for those who had little exposure to choices of clothing.

Then I noticed the aromas. The wind coming off the ocean, the cool air of a crisp fall day, the scent of fine perfumes, the fragrance of a bouquet of roses or lilacs – none of these earthly reminders rivaled the fragrance of heaven. The sweet aromas touched the senses and gave the spirit an upward surge, a lift, which defied any sensation of earthly description.

Next I observed how busy everyone was in heaven. Everyone was working hard, not lounging around grafted to a cloud, and contrary to my expectations, not singing all the time.

Songs had their place, but they were no substitute for the work that was required of the souls in heaven. Work in heaven? Get used to it. The basic work required leaving the concrete and mundane worries of earthly existence and striving toward the spiritual perfection that God expected.

But there was music in heaven. It was not that of an organ, piano or any one instrument. It had elements of the old Gregorian chants, the orchestral music of Bach and Mozart, choral arrangements of Handel, Viennese waltzes of Shubert, old and modern country music of Johnny Cash, jazz, rhythm and blues of New Orleans, hip-hop, rock and roll of Elvis Presley, the Beatles and all other musical forms put together in a miraculous way. It was the most beautiful, soul-stirring, surround sound one could imagine, in no way comparable to any earthly sounds. It vibrated through every part of my body and soul.

When I heard heavenly music, I had to stop everything I was doing. It was impossible to work and listen to the music at the same time. No multi-tasking here! Not that it was forbidden. It was just impossible to do in the presence of that glorious heavenly music.

Another aspect of heaven surprised me. I noticed a few of the saints appeared to be eating. I always had the impression that in heaven food was unnecessary. When I asked about it, my assumption was correct. Food was not required to sustain a physical body. But food could be eaten for the sheer pleasure of it.

Here in heaven, food such as fruits, vegetables, breads and meats were to the body what listening to music was to the soul. Neither food nor music was necessary for existence in heaven, but both were available for the everlasting enjoyment of the residents. And there were no restrictions on what you could eat or how much. I imagined that for some of my friends who had very hearty appetites, this unlimited food supply was heaven enough for them.

I can hear you ask, "What about sexual desires?" They have occupied the minds and bodies of humans ever since time began.

Upon the creation of the world, God implanted in humans and animals the urge to reproduce. Without the enormous sense of pleasure derived from sexual stimulation, propagation of the species would have been in doubt. So the sexual urge had a very real purpose. With millions of inhabitants in heaven, there was clearly no need for further propagation of the species. There were enough folks there already.

The sexual instinct was so powerful that it caused all kinds of havoc. It was also a tremendous source of pleasure, while creating human bonding. It was not easily forgotten by those who were in heaven.

When heaven's inhabitants learned that God eliminated sexual desire from the agenda, many of the newcomers were very disappointed by this news. Some grieved the loss of sexual ecstasy, but given all the other pleasures that heaven provided, over time many accepted this loss.

But other heavenly citizens continued to have dreams and fantasies of earthly sexual behavior. Some even petitioned God in the hope of restoring sexual pleasure to their days in heaven. The first few attempts at this request fell on deaf spiritual ears. But that did not discourage the "Return of Sex" group from continuing their quest for one of Earth's greatest pleasures. Old pleasures die hard.

One of the most alarming things to earthly sensibilities in heaven was the sheer number of inhabitants living there. I was told that there were millions and maybe billions of souls present. That was hard to figure, as I always had the impression that there was a limit to God's grace, and the number of people in heaven would be relatively small.

I remembered what the prophets in the Old Testament, the saints in the New Testament and Jesus Himself, had said about the saved and the damned.

It always seemed to me that the damned would far outnumber the saved. For example, Jesus said that it was far more difficult for a rich man to enter heaven than it was for a camel to go through the eye of a needle, (the latter referring to a small opening in a city wall). Another explanation is that the word the Bible uses for camel may be translated as a "rope" – still hard to thread through a needle. Also, a well known axiom declared that the way to destruction was broad and the road to eternal life narrow, implying that those admitted would be few.

The Bible has a heavy emphasis on the evil in the world; at least that was my impression from my younger days – growing up in the Dutch Christian Reformed Calvinist tradition. Sometimes I think that my religious training was too slanted toward sin, to the neglect of the love and compassion of Jesus. Both in his preaching and in our catechism classes, the minister of my youth always spoke of "heinous sin." At the time, I never knew exactly what that phrase meant. I was familiar with the Ten Commandments. I did not steal – well hardly ever – did not take God's name in vain and generally obeyed the laws of God. It dawned on me that the "dominie" must have been talking about that bothersome and wonderful thing called sex.

The implication of all this emphasis on sin by our minister was that many of us young Calvinists might not be destined for heaven; we might just be headed for the fires of hell, if we didn't shape up.

But as I grew older and lived to reflect on religious ideas, I began to think that maybe, on Earth, we underestimated what God had in mind for humanity in the after life. Perhaps God is far less punitive and much more charitable than we ever imagined.

From what I have seen so far, there are a huge number of people in heaven, many more than I ever imagined. Since I still don't have the answer to this question of how so many got here, I'm going to make a few inquiries to get clarification on this point.

On Earth, I imagined a more homogenous atmosphere in heaven – residents all dressed alike, occupied in praising God all day long, frozen in eternal rest and never required to work in any way. But that was earthly thinking. I keep forgetting heaven is more spiritual and soulful than physical, and what happens here is a far cry from earthly ways.

How different was it? Things were quite unlike I had ever thought. Instead of just a few Old Testament prophets and latter-day saints and believers, heaven was crowded and busy. The inhabitants were not always ready to sing God's praises. As I looked around and assessed the situation, I got the idea that I had arrived at some kind of purgatory, since everyone was working so hard at self-improvement.

My former concept of heaven was that each resident was a fully developed spirit, purified for heaven's sake and able to rest eternally. That would eliminate the need for working so hard and might leave no room for some kind of purgatory. I had to figure out a way to answer this dilemma.

So to clarify the confusion, I made an appointment with St. Peter. I figured him to be the go-to-guy for any accurate information on heaven. Well, that proved to be harder than I thought it would be, since he was continually busy welcoming new residents to heaven.

As I watched St. Peter with his flowing gown, long beard and weathered face, I had a surge of empathy for him. Was God overworking him? He looked stressed and tired. (What? Fatigue in heaven? Yes, none of the souls in heaven had yet reached perfection. They still retained some of their earthly qualities.) So, I was somewhat hesitant to ask him my questions but felt compelled to do so. I had to know.

While St. Peter was taking a deep breath of spiritual air, I caught his eye and asked him about the true nature of heaven. St. Peter was not particularly happy with my questioning. When I came closer to him, he indeed appeared overworked and tired. I suppose if I were constantly greeting all those folks entering heaven, without a break, I would find it exhausting too. But, being the good man who was put in charge of this role by God, he made the effort and reluctantly began talking to me. He surprised me with his pointed questions.

"My son, why do you want to know? Have you no patience? Are you not able to trust God to tell you about heaven in due time? Why do you want to know everything? Others are not bothering me with such things."

I was a bit put off by these questions and remarks, as I pictured St. Peter to be a more cordial fellow, since he had been appointed the official greeter in heaven. But I reconsidered, and thought that he must have his reasons for not answering me immediately. Apparently, even in heaven, the saints get irritable and fatigued.

I began with:

"Is heaven really a purgatory, which requires an indefinite stay for the purpose of purification? Does this depend on the resident's hard work toward the goal of gaining perfection and on the prayers of friends and relatives still on Earth? Or is this some other version of heaven that no saint or prophet ever revealed to us on Earth?"

St. Peter was still not particularly happy with my questions, but being the good man that he is, he gave it another try and began talking to me again.

As we continued to talk, St. Peter became a bit more congenial. Perhaps he empathized with this upstart who had just arrived in the truly unfamiliar realm of heaven. Maybe the Saint recalled arriving here nearly two millennia ago and remembered the questions he had when he was new to the spiritual world. Whatever the reason, his face appeared to relax as he adjusted his robes. I felt a kindly arm gently embracing my shoulder.

"My son," he said, "heaven is not at all what you were told on Earth. When the prophets and saints of old spoke about it, they only had glimpses of heaven from their experiences in dreams and visions. So folks on Earth have no clear idea or concept of where heaven was, who would be there or what would occur there. God purposely obscured the vision of heaven to test the faith of those on Earth. They would have to use wonder, imagination and dreams to form a picture of what heaven was like. The lack of a definitive description of heaven then required *faith* to believe in its existence and *hope* that believers would attain heaven's rewards."

This certainly was a revelation to me. I couldn't help but ask, "Did God plan it this way before the Earth was formed?"

St. Peter looked at me with a beatific smile and said, "From eternity, my son, from eternity."

Then I asked my question directly. "Since everyone is so busy working hard here and not sitting around singing halleluiah choruses, is this a kind of purgatory? Are folks here required to work so hard? What is the point of all this activity? I was under the impression that when we departed Earth, we would have it easy, that we could hang around and finally get some rest. Isn't that what they always talked about, when earthlings spoke of eternal rest?"

St. Peter adjusted his pastoral robes again, took another deep breath of celestial air and said, "No, son, this is no purgatory. It is heaven."

I had to ask, "Then why aren't folks more relaxed and enjoying eternal rest?"

St. Peter groaned. I sensed he was getting tired of me. He twisted his lip in an un-saintly manner. I had a hard time seeing him like that. I expected more of him, although the comments about him in the New Testament do describe him as being irascible at times. He tried to suppress his irritation by replying,

"Son, you are an impatient one, not unlike some other newcomers here. One of the things you must learn is that everything is revealed here in due time, that heavenly time is hard to understand. Look around you and see what is going on. Try to understand that all questions are not answered, not even in heaven. We humans always want to know all the answers, but only God has a monopoly on them. The true nature of heaven will become clearer to you when God wants you to know."

I was not satisfied with that explanation. I felt St. Peter was being a bit patronizing with me. It annoyed me, but I had no alternative than to accept his remarks.

I did take him up on the idea of observing heaven to try to figure out what all the activity was about. I planned to ask him just why there was so much commotion. I tried to make another appointment with him, but he said he was heavily booked, and it would take weeks in heaven time to see him again. I placed it on my instant calendar. I knew I had to get back to St. Peter, but I had to put it off to a time when he was not so busy.

Meanwhile, when I looked around, I readily counted about a dozen large associations that had been formed, and I couldn't wait to visit them and get more details on what they were all doing.

But first, I found out that upon entering heaven, each new resident is lobbied by group members and asked to join the individual sections. This struck me as an odd activity for heaven. I had enough of lobbying on Earth, when my wife was in politics. I was really tired of the crassness and blatant pressure put on her to go along with any particular group's wishes.

I couldn't imagine why God would permit this in heaven. It reminded me of entering college. It was like being rushed for fraternities, invited to their groups, only to be scrutinized to determine whether you measured up to their standards.

Individual members of groups were extolling the virtues of joining their particular association. I found it rather disturbing of these heavenly residents to be acting so much like earthly people. I had hoped for something more spiritual, ecstatic and blissful. To be asked to join a club seemed too mundane for my taste, but, then again, I was never much of a joiner on Earth and preferred the isolation of individual effort rather than the comfort and validation of group support.

Well, enough of that. As I look into the situation, I will tell you about some of the groups and what they were so preoccupied with. It may surprise you.

"Thought is the labor of the intellect, Reverie its pleasure."

Victor Hugo, *Les Miserables*

CHAPTER 2

My early religious training has me focused and preoccupied with these questions about eternity and heaven. It has a grip on me, and it will not let me go. So I am compelled to tell this story, as I imagine it to be. But before describing more of what I experienced in my dream of heaven, let me take a short journey back to a sentimental and memorable vignette from my childhood. It will give you a clue as to my curiosity about heaven, of what existence may be like in the life hereafter.

*****

In my reverie, I can see myself, at age ten, sitting on a hilltop with a boyhood friend named Rich. I can hear the fire whistles of the town beneath the hill, the very same sounds that I hear today, as I live only a few miles away. As we sit overlooking the scene, vistas of the flat plain that extends to the Hudson River and New York City come to view.

When I was growing up, celery farms with rich, dark soil covered much of the nearby valley. Today the farms are gone, replaced with parking lots and the massive shopping centers in the New Jersey suburb of Paramus. As Rich and I look toward the horizon, through the haze of the late afternoon, we can make out the skyline of New York City. The top half of the double towers holding the suspension bridge of the George Washington Bridge are visible, like two giants holding an unseen object. The spire of the Empire State Building seems to be touching the sky. The World Trade Center has not yet been constructed.

A few years later, New York City was to become "the city," where my brother and I spent many hours at ice skating rinks winning races in short track speed skating. Still later, I attended medical school in New York, and stood for my medical license and training in psychiatry.

But none of this was in my wildest dreams as I sat with my friend overlooking the valley below. The house where my wife, children and I would later live had not yet been built. The local hospital, where I would later spend much time working as a psychiatrist, had not yet been conceived by those who gave birth to its construction.

Rich and I are sitting on the uncut grass that covers the hill. The aroma is sweet. It is summertime and warm, but not hot in the humid, stifling way like New Jersey can be in July or August. We had just hiked in the woods along the foothills of the Ramapo Mountains, the first hills that can be seen from the incoming ships entering New York harbor from the Atlantic Ocean.

Nearby are the rolling fields known to us kids as the "hay-fields," the local cow pasture, where our youthful baseball and football fantasies are played out.

Our town lacked any of the manicured athletic playing fields readily seen now all over suburbia. On those few acres of cow pasture, our physical skills were constantly challenged by maneuvering around the new and old circular "cow flops" that were randomly distributed on our makeshift athletic field. Our Levi's (jeans came later) seldom escaped the crud and the persistent aroma of cow manure. Our mothers patiently cleaned up the mess that we made.

I still remember with pleasure the rough and tumble of football, the exhilaration of an open field tackle, the thrill of a one-handed catch from a perfectly thrown spiral and the attempt to run through the line of scrimmage, defying the tackling skills of my friends to bring me down.

When my brother, Bert, bought me a leather football helmet for my birthday, I felt very special, like a real football player. I was the only one wearing a helmet, just like the college football star Tommy Harmon, whose picture hung on my bedroom wall.

*****

Hearing the fire alarm whistles today, there is something hauntingly comforting about them. Baoom, baoom, baoom. How could such a weird sound be in any way comforting? Maybe it's my friend, with whom I had a bond and felt comforted, as one who is understood, a friend with whom I could validate life's experience. I don't think that the sound, by itself, would be comforting, had I sat there alone on that hill so many years ago.

Do we experience life more in the presence of others? Or is life best appreciated in the lonely hours, free of the distracting elements of others? Although I need both the friends and the time alone for reflection, many of my friends seem to need people around them constantly, as though their spirits are not elevated by the silence of being alone. Many people do not appear to need the calm the spirit gains from the soul's retreat from human interaction. And why the difference? Is it all variation in personality or family background? Is it all genetic?

Most of the friends of my youth were action-oriented. They liked sports. My nephew, Dan, the same age as me, was tall and slender. He was excellent at baseball and basketball, and played with dexterity on teams in high school.

I had difficulty with eye-hand coordination with small objects like baseballs. I wore eyeglasses from age eight or nine on. And having been hit on the head by a pitched ball early on, I was forever fearful of and a failure at baseball. The roughhouse of football appealed to me, but our small school had no football team. Besides, I was preoccupied with riding my one-speed racing bike in training for ice skating races.

Early on, I noticed that some of my friends were not afraid to take risks, whether sledding down a dangerous hill past cross streets that had no stop signs, or driving cars dangerously fast. One day I was in a car with a friend named Louie when he sailed through a stop sign at thirty miles an hour. I was alarmed and yelled at him, but he simply thought it was fun.

Another time, I was in a car with a few friends. We approached a railroad crossing, which at that time had no crossing gates – only a flashing red light. We could see a train coming down upon us. The driver, Gary, took one look at the light of the approaching train and proceeded to cross the track. Reacting to his recklessness, we shouted at him, "You jerk! What are, you stupid? We could have been killed!"

His reply: "Yeah, we lose more trains that way." Our anger was followed by a big sigh of relief, as we continued on to The Barn, a local restaurant, where we satisfied our ravenous appetites for hamburgers and ice cream.

Through a remarkable coincidence a few years ago, I met a friend of Gary's, named Jack, who was a psychologist. We met at a psychiatric meeting in Park City, Utah. Gary and he were colleagues living in California. After a short time talking with Jack, I realized that he knew Gary. Jack then told me that, at the age of seventy-five, Gary spends his free time parachuting out of airplanes, just for the fun of it. I thought about this and concluded that nothing changes when it comes to character traits. Gary lived dangerously when he was young, and this trait seemed to continue throughout his later years. Qualities seen early on in life tend to persist.

In my high school years, there were those among us who

tended to be more cautious, more reflective, suffered more guilt and were less inclined to take on the imaginative risks of childhood. I was one of them. Some of us could have been described today as "nerds," engaged mostly in intellectual pursuits.

Looking back, I still can't believe that a group of us, when we were in college, spent Sunday afternoons studying the weighty religious tome *Calvin's Institutes* of our own volition. Why weren't we out having fun like most college-aged students?

Back in high school, other friends were hanging out at the local ice cream store across from our high school. They were smoking Camel, Chesterfield or Lucky Strike cigarettes, flicking the ashes with deft fingers or dangling them from their mouths like famous movie stars. On the sly, they drank Pabst Blue Ribbon Beer in defiance of our elders, enjoying the forbidden pleasures of our time. My friend Rich was one of these guys. I later learned that some of the adults in our community, staunch members of the church, had a penchant for alcohol too, but were usually secretive about their drinking.

A number of my friends were good students as well as capable athletes, closely following the traditional line. I was one of these "good boys."

But one could seldom predict what would happen to those we knew in high school. Our school was a private "Christian" school run by Dutch immigrants from the late 1800s and early 1900s.

These hard working, religious folk were employed in the silk mills and the tool and dye factories in Paterson, N.J.; others became carpenters, bakers, painters, electricians, gardeners or managers of local mom and pop stores. Parents saved the few dollars they had and paid the tuition for their children's "Christian education." If they could not afford it, the Dutch Christian Reformed Church provided the funds. I never knew whether my parents had to resort to this means to support my education.

Although the school was private, it had fewer accoutrements than a modern prison. The school had one playground that consisted of macadam and concrete. Another was a sloped, uneven sandlot with many interspersed weeds.

We had none of the educational or cultural frills. It was a stripped-to-the-bone institution. I don't even remember a library in our grade school. The richest source of learning was the extent of theological and spiritual training we received. Oh yes, we had plenty of Bibles and a few excellent teachers.

Given this background of staunch Calvinism taught in our school, I found it hard to understand the relative disinterest in religion among many of my boyhood friends. A few of us, having a natural bent toward reflection, were often visited by recurring thoughts and questions about the deeper meaning of life. Others were remarkably free of worries about their existence.

My friend Rich was one of those guys who took life as it came. He was always ready for a laugh or a trick played to perfection on one of his friends.

He was not intimidated by the school principal or the prevailing authorities. I remember him telling us of an encounter with the high school principal, whom Rich imitated with the skill of a practiced actor. When called into that hallowed office for multiple minor infractions, the principal, Mr. Bos gave Rich a life lesson. While spreading his index and middle finger to illustrate the point, he said,

"Rich, there are two paths in life, two paths Rich – and Rich; you're going down the wrong path, the wrong path, Rich. The wrong path will get you nowhere but trouble, Rich."

Rather than feeling corrected by this stern admonition, Rich thought it was funny and enjoyed mimicking the principal in telling us about it. We, of course, roared with laughter after his telling of the encounter with the principal.

He pushed the limits of our narrow existence, and we were enlivened by his stories, if only by proxy. I not only admired his aggression, but also that he did not fear reprisal. Given the restrictions under which we lived at that time, he stood out as the exception. There was a side of him that I admired, though I was unable to make his behavior a part of my daily routine.

There was another part of Rich's life that was outside of my experience. He was one of five boys in his family, watched and prayed over by their saintly, widowed mother, a strongly religious woman. She was admired by her friends, and she volunteered in the African-American missions in Paterson. With finances low, her boys were all forced to work at an early age.

I remember vividly, as if it were yesterday, a scene that occurred each Monday morning while I was eating breakfast. A knock on our back door signaled the presence of my friend Rich. Was he ready to play a game before school started or did he have other things in mind? No. Rich stood at the door with pencil and pad in hand, poised to take the weekly order from my mother for meats and cold cuts from the local butcher shop.

Each morning Rich had the unenviable task of calling on customers to take orders, which were later delivered to the homes in the community. Rich had to get up early before attending school to complete his chores.

These were the days when few families had cars for shopping and vendors came to the house to sell all kinds of things. I remember Mr. Kaptyn, who had a dry goods store in our half-square-mile town of Prospect Park. He made the rounds about once a month to sell his wares. He was very engaging. He showed me some card tricks, which I still remember to this day.

One time, my little female fox terrier, Patty, was missing. Mr. Kaptyn just happened to find her and brought her back the next day. Some weeks later my Patty had puppies.

I was just old enough to know how puppies came into this world. "Aha! They're not fooling me," I thought. "Now I know why Patty was missing."

I soon forgot about the adult deception when the fun of playing with the puppies overwhelmed me, like the joy of newfound playmates.

On other occasions, a blind man arrived at my home from Paterson on a bus, accompanied by a young boy. He sold shoe laces, string, needles, safety pins, yarn, glue, pencils and other assorted small items. He was like a walking Dollar Store of today, except that the items cost a nickel or a dime at that time. Other vendors included the coal man – quite important before the era of gas and oil to heat homes – the iceman – prior to the invention of refrigerators, and the dependable early morning delivery of milk by the milkman. My brother Jack was a milkman, and I often accompanied him on his deliveries during the summer; he allowed me to drive the milk truck from one brief stop to another. At age fifteen, that was a thrill.

On several mornings each week, Mr. Hagedorn, the peddler, shouted out his presence for mothers to come to the street to purchase fruits, vegetables and canned goods. About once a month, the "junk man" came around with his horse and wagon looking for objects cast aside from homes in the neighborhood, which he could sell in Paterson. He always looked like he needed a good night's sleep. The neighborhood kids called him "sleepy Sam."

All these characters that enriched my childhood years ago are absent from my current neighborhood, replaced by the impersonal strip malls and large shopping malls of our day. Only a fragment of the old days still exists in the small delis and grocery stores, where I can chat with the employees on a first name basis.

So when Rich came in the morning to my house, not to play

but to work, to earn a few dollars for his family, I saw another side of him. While I admired him for his efforts to help his family, I did not envy his early morning rounds.

But to me, the most admirable aspect of Rich's talents was his ability to meet the challenge of the playground – the duel of fisticuffs – so common among elementary school boys. Although I enjoyed football and even wrestling, I had no inclination or taste for serious physical combat. I clearly "chickened out" when it came to punching someone after a provocation. Not Rich. When taunted or pushed too hard, Rich was always ready to engage in a fight, which by virtue of school rules had to be off-site – across the street from school property.

We all knew that fighting was not permitted on school grounds. And if any of us were caught fighting on the school playground, we had to contend with the stern Dutch elementary school principal, whose wrath many of us feared. He was the ultimate disciplinarian. In retrospect, he was the perfect personification and archetype for the God we Calvinists were taught to fear.

One day, for whatever reason, Rich and a classmate, Bob, were determined to work out their mutual anger over insults long since forgotten. A formal boxing match was scheduled during our lunch hour. A trail of onlookers, mostly boys, sauntered over to the empty lot across from the school to watch the fight. The tension in the crowd grew, as these fights were not an everyday event.

The two boys stood opposite each other putting on their fiercest fighting masks. Rich looked the toughest, with a ragged shirt and soiled trousers that had seen better days. He wore moccasins, relics from playing cowboys and Indians. He had removed his eyeglasses.

Bob was dressed in a shirt, clean pants and sneakers. He looked more like the traditional schoolboy. The two antagonists stood with arms raised in the fighter's pose. Neither registered fear on their faces, only anger. Fists were clenched and ready to go. Then the time-honored tradition was observed. One of the onlookers placed a chip of wood on Rich's shoulder. With a look of defiance, Bob hit the chip off with his hand, signaling that the fight was officially started.

The contenders danced around in a circle, jabbing at the air, but landing no punches. They continued their movements, looking for the chance to land a blow. A bit of shadow boxing warmed up the contestants.

Suddenly, fists flew to the body and to the head. Bob got in a good right to the jaw. Rich countered with a punch to the stomach, followed by a left hook to Bob's nose. Bob was stunned, but he recovered. He lunged at Rich and got in a roundhouse punch to the stomach. Then Rich landed another jab to Bob's nose.

Immediately, Bob withdrew, holding his nose, from which bright red blood began to flow.

Almost as soon as it had begun, the fight was over. The crowd was obviously disappointed at the short duration of the match. Rich was presumed the winner as Bob had stopped fighting.

None of the eager observers applauded or congratulated the winner. We had not really taken sides. Rich and Bob were both our friends. But they had a disagreement and needed to work it out. Bob had only time to stop the bleeding before arriving in class. Neither teachers nor the principal ever heard of the contest. The fight was over, and we all walked back to class, the two boys having successfully resolved the tension between them. It all seemed like an unnecessary part of growing up. But the less aggressive among us tended to walk away from such conflicts or talked our way out of them.

I have often wondered why I preferred the latter route to the open conflict that some of my peers seemed to enjoy. I have heard some of my current friends say that they love a good fight.

Of course, they are referring to a verbal fight, not fisticuffs. Even verbal fights turn me off, although I can perform adequately in this emotional arena if sufficiently provoked.

Reflecting on the differences in how people view physical or verbal fighting, it seems to me that it has much to do with temperament. There are those predisposed to the more pugilistic ways of resolving problems, while others take the more conciliatory route. While I admired the aggression of my friend Rich, the fist fighter I knew in my youth, I do not think he was ever envious of my peacemaking and problem-solving nature.

Many years have slipped by. Rich dropped out of school, but later returned and went to college, as he was always very bright. I recently came across Rich's picture in my wife Marge's college yearbook. They graduated the same year from Montclair State College. Below his college yearbook picture was the note, "He sees social significance in everything."

It was no surprise then that Rich became a social studies teacher beloved by his students. Later, as a teachers' union negotiator, I can only imagine that he was an effective force for raising teachers' salaries and benefits. I am certain that he was also a thorn in the side of school administrators.

While still in college, Rich invited me to a school event at Montclair State College. There he introduced me to Marge, who was the president of the local chapter of an organization called Intervarsity Christian Fellowship. The following year we met again in New York at a similar gathering. Two years later, she and I were married. I have always been grateful to Rich for inviting me to that first meeting.

Over fifty years have elapsed since then. In recent years, I had lunch with Rich a few times. The food was good, but the hours reminiscing about the past were even more delicious.

A couple of years ago, my boyhood friend Rich died suddenly of a heart attack while riding a bike. As with other friends, I regret that I did not spend more time with him remembering and reflecting about our boyhood years and talking about what life has meant to each of us. Marge and I went to his memorial service.

In spite of all our religious training in grade school and high school and all the church attendance throughout our college years, no reference was made at the memorial by the speakers to any spiritual sentiments. There was but one exception. One of Rich's brothers, John, read a psalm. No speaker mentioned Rich having a religious life, and no one made any reference to the after life in any way.

The lack of religious comments surprised me somewhat, although I had known that Rich did not follow any faith tradition.

But, in spite of this, I like to think that my childhood friend Rich made it to heaven – still possessing his earthly personality, continuing to wrestle with God like Jacob in an attempt to find some meaning for his life on Earth. Could that be one of the things we will all do in heaven – discuss life on Earth with God and challenge God like Job in order to discover why we were put on this planet?

Bob, the other playground fighter, went on to college and Bible school and eventually became an evangelist. Who could have guessed the journey either of my friends took? Who could have predicted any of the paths we ended up taking?

My high school graduation yearbook predicted I would become a minister of the Gospel. Well, I am glad they were wrong. Although I had a fleeting thought about entering a seminary while in college, I found my life as a psychiatrist very satisfying. Helping others as a physician in the counseling role met my needs. I never regretted the decision.

Over the years since childhood, I have wondered, intermittently, what happened to my friends who did not live the religious life that was taught to us as children. What made Bob become an evangelist and Rich an agnostic? And what of their fate in the eternal? Does being an evangelist give one a ticket to heaven? Does living life as a teacher devoted to children with little attention to existential issues result in eternal hell? I have trouble with these alternatives.

How can God conceive of eternal damnation for the humans he has created? On Earth, punishment is deemed helpful in the hope of rehabilitation. Of what value would it be for God to punish eternally? These are some of the questions that I have had growing up in my world – a comfortable culture of relative peace, compared to what most humans throughout the world experience.

"Most humans are enthralled with their own self-importance, while God sees us as fragile creatures, all of whom need His help."

Richard Roukema

CHAPTER 3

Back in heaven, I began looking around at the various groups. I began thinking about which one to join. There were many groups and all had their initial appeal. But before I arrived at any decision about which group to join, the light bulb of comic strip fame suddenly went off over my head. Why do I have to be a group member at all? Or, maybe I could join several groups and do something special as well.

As I told you, on Earth I was never attracted to joining groups. I grew up in a very large family with seven siblings, and it always seemed to me that there were too many people around (especially with only one bathroom). So maybe that's why I preferred doing things on my own, experiencing things that were different.

For example, in my early teens, every guy I knew had a "balloon" tire bike, except me. I had a one-speed racing bike, which followed me to three different colleges in various parts of the country. How many people do you know who went to three different colleges? How many are psychiatrists? Okay, different. Did I join a fraternity in college or medical school? No.

Much later, did I associate myself with one of the various psychoanalytic schools? Yes, in order to obtain psychoanalytical training, I had to align myself with a training facility. But was I a Freudian, a Jungian, an Adlerian or any of the subsequent groups that came into existence? No, different. Allegiance to particular groups has never been my forté. Well, not entirely, as I did belong to professional groups, like the American Medical Association and the American Psychiatric Association, but membership in these groups was necessary in order to be considered legitimate.

So on impulse, instead of concentrating on which group to join here in heaven, I thought up this idea. Why not become a roving reporter in heaven? But as I ruminated on the reporter gig, I had some misgivings about this role. I didn't think God would accept reporters in heaven. He had heard enough about the paparazzi of earthly fame. Why would He want them dogging Him here?

So, after mulling it over, I came up with a title – a role – GOD'S AMBASSADOR for GROUP INTEGRITY and CONSENSUS (GAGIC). (In order to be with it, I still felt the earthly need to have an acronym).

I had heard a rumor that God was concerned about these diverse groups in heaven getting along with each other, and of course, God wanted integrity. So I thought that maybe an ambassador would come in handy to keep God informed as to how each group was doing, and how the group relations were playing out.

As you know well, God didn't need me for this role at all. By His very nature, He is omniscient. No person or group could delude Him as to His intent or ultimate goal. But I hoped that He would humor me and give me the honor of being His personal ambassador.

In thinking along these lines, we mortals continue to reason in earthly ways. That is, if someone is in charge of an organization, a government or a nation, he must need an underling or a deputy to carry out his plan.

In my earthly travels abroad some years ago, my wife (then a member of the U.S. Congress) and I met many ambassadors. I thought they had interesting jobs. They lived in wonderful surroundings, met with world leaders and never had to worry about such mundane things as the laundry, housekeeping or "What are we having for dinner tonight, dear?" Of course, none of these amenities would apply in heaven, but it would still be a great honor to be God's ambassador. After all, this is a dream.

The question was how to get an audience with the Almighty and plug my idea. He was not that readily available in person or in spirit. I first thought of e-mail, but why would God have to resort to such earthly means of communication? Besides, I hadn't seen a computer since being in heaven.

How about reaching Him by prayer? That consistently worked on Earth as long as you were serious about your prayers and not bothering Him with micro-managing the Universe (like praying for good weather, great wealth or your favorite NFL football team).

Well, I decided to take the direct approach. I thought of contacting St. Peter again, but after my last experience with him, I wondered if that was such a good idea. Then the angel Gabriel came to mind. He was known for sending messages to earthlings. But I figured he would be too hard to find, since he was always going down to Earth to do his job.

With a feeling of resignation, I again went to St. Peter. When I approached him, he had that "not you again" look on his face, He appeared so fierce, I thought he was going to bounce me off a cloud and let me fall to Earth again.

When I gave him my proposal asking to be God's ambassador to heaven, he laughed and said, "Hey, look here, you're a newcomer. What right do you have to ask God for a special job?

God never made me an ambassador for Him. How could He possibly give you the job?"

That annoyed me for some reason, and by that time, I was beginning to feel like Jacob or Moses when they tussled with God. I had the audacity to challenge the Saint by asking, "With all due respect, St. Peter, did you ever ask God if you could represent Him in heaven as an ambassador?"

He was taken aback by my impertinence. He shook his head in disgust. The atmosphere had a heavy feel, the smell of a loud, "No!" from St. Peter. But, after considerable verbal fumbling, he had to concede that he had never thought of the idea of asking God if he could be His ambassador. Besides, every joke I ever heard about heaven began with St. Peter greeting folks as they entered the pearly gates. That job kept him busy enough. Since I had the implied copyright (or was it the idea-right) on the position of ambassador, St. Pete grudgingly submitted my concept to God the same day. In heaven, as on planet Earth, things can move fast if you are well connected.

It seemed to be only minutes before I was asked to appear before the Almighty to render my credentials for the job. Minutes, hours, days—they all feel the same here.

Contrary to earthly concepts of God, He did not look like a bearded old man or a mature woman. He had no bodily form that is familiar on Earth. Was he like a cloud? Only in that His form kept changing. At once, He was a bright light and then a dark cloud, then an array of colors. I saw that it was impossible to describe Him adequately. That makes sense. After all, the Scriptures say, "God is Spirit." And how does one describe a spirit?

Despite our efforts to put God in earthly form, I concluded that this is not God's way of showing Himself. He did not permit any earthly expression of His appearance. He was simply a heavenly presence.

With deference, and mustering up as much appropriate humility as I could, I offered to God that I had good interviewing skills and was an excellent listener and note taker. On occasion, I could even do a cartoon of what was happening in a group if that were necessary, as photographs were prohibited in heaven.

Knowing all things, God did not have to ask for my resume, but following earthly protocols, as He often did in biblical days with His Chosen Ones, He humored me and went through the motions. In an instant, I became the first, and to my knowledge only, ambassador in heaven. This is a role I never dreamed of on Earth. I suspect that we are in for many surprises in heaven, about which we mortals have no knowledge.

I was so overcome I hardly knew what to say. In my excitement, I fell from one cloud to another. Finally, I regained my composure and thanked God for His grace. I vowed to do my best to inform Him about what was happening in all of the groups on a daily basis. I didn't know which group to visit first.

This being heaven, there are no emergencies and nothing is urgent. One activity is no more important than another. So, unlike Earth, I could simply relax and take my time.

Ah yes, time: that Earth-bound concept. I fully expected it to be the same linear concept in heaven. But one moment flowed into another. Sometimes time flew backward and at other times forward. One could not make dates or appointments with people and depend on them being there. It was like swimming in cross currents, swirling about one another, like a boat without a rudder. Things constantly changed.

I kept making appointments with individuals and groups in heaven. Many times they worked out, and at other times I had to try again.

But, like so many other things here, you eventually became used to it. You accepted the fluidity of heaven. Things do not have to be done on time or in a specific way. But somehow, in the chaos of it all, everything works out for the best in the end. In heaven, persons have to relax any obsessive-compulsive tendencies they have left over from their days on Earth.

Let's go visit some of the groups I saw in my dream of heaven. As we go on this adventure, you may begin to think of which group would appeal to you should you enter heaven's gate.

"The prophets and saints have eternal honor in God's heaven. On Earth our honors are momentary."

Richard Roukema

CHAPTER 4

The groups in heaven were divided into many categories. I was taken by the similarity to those on Earth. It was as though the inhabitants of heaven could not dispel the old habits of their former home. They had to do similar things in some way, with minor alterations. The groups that had formed were all too familiar.

For example, the prophets of the Old Testament liked to gather in the OLD SOULS' AUTHORITIVE CLUB (OSAC), much like the senior citizens clubs that I remembered on Earth. The members seemed to be very relaxed and were not working hard at anything. Most of them were dressed in the old biblical styles with robes and sandals. They seemed to prefer beards, but they did not look old; hardly anyone had gray hair. They were in comfortable surroundings with attractive huts and abundant trees and wild life that seemed remarkably peaceful.

Here in heaven, the lions were as friendly as the lambs. The eagles and other raptors were not flying around looking for prey. All wildlife seemed to be fulfilled and have adequate supplies for all their needs, which were few. When looking at this scene, I was struck with an overwhelming sense of tranquility.

Whatever task had been given to the old-timers had been completed, except for some teaching and consulting work. There was nothing urgent to do. No one was in a hurry. All was right with heaven for the OSAC that I saw.

I learned that there were a number of members of this group who had attained the age of 200 to 300 years on Earth. But no one had ever come close to Methuselah, who was revered here for having lived the longest recorded span of 969 years. Each heavenly year, he was again appointed president, in what seemed an endless job. I learned that Abraham, Isaac, and Jacob were there, as well as Elijah and Elisha. I thought that one day I would want to spend some time talking to these biblical figures about their lives on Earth.

A kindly soul pointed out Noah to me. Now there is someone with whom I would like to reminisce. I have so many questions for him – like how did he manage all those animals, birds and reptiles with their food and water needs and the stench of their daily waste discharge? How did he cope with the loss of all his friends? How did he discover he liked wine enough to pass out from it? Wouldn't these things be interesting to discuss?

I also discovered that all of the major and minor prophets were present. Ah, yes, Joseph, he was there too. In the Bible stories about him that I learned in childhood, he was one of my heroes.

Somehow, I didn't think we needed leaders to direct groups in heaven, but I guess I was wrong; even a bunch of free-flying spirits need guidance. I was eager to hear what these old-timers did and what they talked about all day long.

After a prolonged search for the big man in charge, I finally found Methuselah. At first I did not know what to say. How does one relate to a man who has lived more than ten lifetimes on

Earth? I approached him gingerly and introduced myself to him. To my surprise, I found him to be very cordial and gracious. He welcomed me into the group and introduced me around.

The looks of compassion, the kindness and the openness of these sages was, at first, somewhat astonishing. I simply didn't expect this degree of friendliness, as they made every attempt to help me feel comfortable. I don't remember the elderly always being that cordial to strangers on Earth. Rather, I recall that when encountering a group of elderly citizens, there frequently was some apprehension, as though I had entered their space or disturbed their routine and made them anxious.

I expected the old-timers in heaven to be less friendly and more patronizing. But not so, they were as pleasant as I could imagine.

I concluded that the sages of old had matured to the point of losing their defensiveness and no longer had anything to prove. It occurred to me that even on Earth, I had met a few elderly folks who were much like this. They had fought the good fight, had no reason to be defensive and had a mature, reflective view of the world and the universe. I always aspired to that kind of state, but I'm afraid I didn't quite make it before reaching heaven.

As Methuselah took me around, I heard many welcomes and kindly greetings. Some of the members of this group were discussing events that were happening on Earth. Others were talking about groups in heaven. I overheard one gathering wondering how it was possible for some of the groups, like the politicians' or lawyers' associations, to always be engaged in one controversy or another. Here in the OLD SOULS' AUTHORITIVE CLUB, there was none of that. If it ever existed, it had long ago been discarded and replaced by enlightened conversations that were only helpful and encouraging.

As far as I could see, this group had reached a level close to or at perfection. Of course, they had had a long time to attain such an exalted station in heaven. And perhaps God gave them a special dispensation because of their revered lives on Earth.

I soon noticed one of the group leaders. He turned out to be Hosea, one of the Old Testament prophets – a man of questionable morality during his time on Earth. He appeared to be mature and in a position of leadership. He had a radiance about him that belied my previous vision of him. Like many of the others, Hosea had a neatly trimmed beard, was dressed in a flowing white robe and wore sandals.

I wanted to ask him about the elderly statesmen and their experiences in heaven. But I first had to clarify a question I had about what he wrote eons ago in the Bible.

"Tell me, sir. You must have been here a long time. I read in the Bible, the book with your name, about some of your adventures on Earth, like the time God commanded you to have a child with a prostitute. Quite frankly, I have a problem understanding that command, but maybe you can explain it to me."

"Well, son," he replied, "you are not the first one to be caught up with the Bible's account of me. The reference to which you refer is not factual but metaphorical. God was very disappointed by what Israel was doing in regard to worshiping Him. They had turned to other Gods, the way men on Earth turn to prostitutes instead of to their legitimate wives. So don't be put off by those verses. Much of what I wrote about is in that same vein, God's reaction to Israel's turn to idolatry. It was a common theme and concern of God, as His people repeatedly turned from Him to other gods."

For the moment, I was satisfied with that rendition of the beginning of Hosea's book. So I went on to another question.

"Let me as ask you this. I am curious about the group in which you walk. Here in heaven, the prophets of old seem to be finished with their work. Tell me, what was the nature of this group, especially when the members first came here, and how have they changed?"

Hosea replied, "When we were neophyte entrants into heaven, we did not know what to expect. After a short time here, we came upon the angel Gabriel, who seemed like he knew his way all around God's heaven. So we asked him what to do and how to behave. He said we were not constrained to be anything special. He said that we should sit around and discuss our role as senior statesmen.

"We were not expected to do much besides help those who would be arriving in heaven as the years went by. So, in effect, we were heaven's counselors or pastors, much like on Earth. We were often asked to go to groups, such as the doctors' or lawyers' group or any of the other associations and counsel them on their special problems.

"As you might imagine, we took to this idea, because it was familiar to us. However, there was a big difference. We became expert pastors, free of sin and we never made any errors in our counseling. Of course, this was only possible because of God's grace."

"Have you felt satisfied with this role or do you sometimes get restless with the newcomers, who may have exalted expectations?" I asked.

"Yes, some of the new entrants to heaven can sometimes be a problem. But they are a challenge, and we enjoy our work. We are all completely attached to our task and deem it God's choice for us. There is nothing we would rather do, and we are grateful. It is a gift from God," said Hosea.

This just felt like it was too good to be true. So I dared to ask the next question.

"In the early days of your journey in heaven, was everything so quiet and peaceful? Were there ever any in the group unhappy with their role? And did any of the members want to leave and join other groups here in heaven?"

I am certain that Hosea had to explain this to others in the past before me. He took a deep breath, as though he was becoming a bit tired of answering these questions yet again.

"At first we did not know what God had in mind for us, so we talked to the angels. You understand that although there were many inhabitants here before we arrived, they did not seem to know much about what was going on here. You may recall that St. Peter, who later became God's official greeter in heaven, hadn't arrived yet. The angels clued us in to what God planned for us as the pastors, advisors and sages of heaven. This role pleased many in the group, but there were a few holdouts, who thought that they deserved more of a leadership role, since they were among the first of the biblical characters to arrive. But since there was no possibility of revolt in heaven, except for Lucifer, the devil himself, they soon softened their views and folded into the consensus of the group and followed along as God willed it."

Well, it was clear from his remarks that this was one group that could not be improved upon. So I thanked them for the visit and prepared to leave. I vowed to return in order to talk to some of my favorite heroes, especially Joseph and Noah. I made a spirited leap to another group.

On the way I thought about how the OSAC might be a group that appealed to me. I wondered what it would be like to be with them all day. The problem was that I did not qualify by virtue of age or experience and, oh yes, I had serious doubts about my sage-hood. Maybe after a few centuries in heaven, they might grant me admission, if I kept my spiritual robes clean and did my job to God's satisfaction.

Having just made that statement, it occurs to me that it's extremely hard not to think along Earth's traditional ways, as though if I do the "right" thing, I will be rewarded. The Bible states this idea in many ways and at other times says that, with God, we cannot earn our way to heaven through good works;

faith gets us there through His grace. The latter is the belief of most Protestant Christians following the biblical interpretations of Martin Luther and other reformers.

Could it be that in heaven we will not be rewarded for our good works? Wow! It's so difficult to make the transition to heaven's way of thinking – no, not a way of *thinking* but the way of *being – a spiritual being.*

Clearly, there was little for me to report to God about the old-timers' group (OSAC). They had it all together. Of course, God knew this. He didn't need me to tell Him. But I made my report anyway. Just part of the job, I thought.

"Search thine own heart. What paineth thee in others in thyself may be."

John Greenleaf Whittier, *The Chapel of the Hermits*

CHAPTER 5

As I moved around at will, I observed a group that seemed a bit stuffy. Immediately I felt very unwelcome with them, since each subdivision of the group seemed to have a language all its own. It was not a foreign tongue as I could understand every word. It was more of a religio-speak. If you did not use the words they expected to hear, in the manner familiar to them, they looked down on you, as though you were an inferior creature and really did not deserve to be in heaven with them.

In conversation with these folks, you had to acknowledge God in everything and never fail to mention His name, even when referring to the most insignificant event in your life. Otherwise, they looked at you in a condescending manner, as though you simply did not get it, whatever "it" was supposed to be.

They gave me the impression they thought they were the best of God's chosen people, deserving of a special place in heaven. It reminded me of some groups on Earth, each of whom knew that it had all the answers to life's greatest questions. In lower celestial regions they were called fundamentalists, whether their beliefs had originated from Islamic, Christian, Judaic faiths or from Buddhism, Hinduism, Taoism or whatever. Here in heaven, they were called the EXCLUSIVE ISMS CLUB (EIC).

Each division of this group believed that there was only one way to think about God and existential matters and each was quick to criticize those who differed on a host of issues. It seemed strange that even here in heaven, these diverse groups continued their isolated ways of viewing things.

Some in the EIC stressed the ritual of prayers several times a day as required for the faithful. Others insisted on religious services weekly with prayer meetings in between. Some worshiped in a quiet way in meditative states. Others danced and waved their hands and sang loudly, or chanted religious passages while rocking back and forth. Still another group felt it had to kneel in prayer several times every celestial day. And each group felt that it had the final answer to how one should worship God to the exclusion of all other views.

I noticed that each ISM was separated from the others by a huge wall. I was cautioned by one of the prophets to be very quiet when walking among these ISMS, as each had the temerity to believe that it was the only group elected to be in heaven.

This kind of prejudice toward others did not fit well with my concept of the nature of heaven.

But hear this: it was not their earthly beliefs that made them eligible for this particular group, since they differed so much on ultimate truth. What qualified each of them was their exclusivity, the fact that they allowed no quarter to doubt or differential thinking on the part of their members.

Wow! That was a surprise. I could not imagine them all being in the same exclusive club. I never dreamed that I would see these disparate groups all assembled in one place in heaven.

For a moment, a nasty earthly thought passed through my mind – maybe they deserved each other. I planned to spend some time with the ISMS in an attempt to discover how they were faring in this isolated state, unable to get along with each other. As you know, on Earth that's exactly how they live.

I looked around for someone who seemed knowledgeable about the group. This was no easy task. I had little success at first. Each person I spoke to could not figure out why the other group divisions were in heaven. Each distinct section seemed to think that it had earned the right to be in heaven exclusively. They walked around with their noses in the air, stubbornly ignoring anyone who did not view things exactly as they did or did not use their version of religio-speak.

They were dressed in a variety of ways, ranging from robes and sandals to orthodox black clothes, hats and long hair. Others were dressed informally, but some insisted in dressing in their earthly Sabbath day or Sunday best.

I was beginning to despair on getting the real scope on this situation. I decided to talk with a man at random. His name was Joe. Maybe he could clarify some things for me. Joe was dressed in a clerical robe, as though he had attained a celestial position and complete knowledge, the last word in truth. His brow was taut with furrows deep enough to plant corn in. He had such a patronizing attitude; I was surprised that he even agreed to talk with me.

I approached him and asked, "Tell me, sir, the members in this group seem so disparate, so different. How did you all get to join the same group?"

Joe shook his head and looked at me as though I was really an inferior creature. But he indulged me and replied in a condescending voice:

"I know why I'm here, because on Earth I searched for the truth and I found the Lord. I was born again. I followed my faith in Him, and it turned out to be all true. I got what I expected – my reward in heaven. Some of my friends arrived here the same way, through faith in the Scriptures.

"But I don't know what these other weirdoes are doing here, those who have the devil's version of faith. I know that there is only one way to get to heaven, and I found it. I don't know what's going to happen to these other strange people. I guess God will send them to hell eventually. I think God put them here to show them what they will be missing, and how wrong they were about rejecting the one true faith."

I was amazed at his arrogance and felt I had to confront him.

"Joe, how do you know you were privy to the absolute final religious truth on Earth?"

He looked me straight in the eye and said, as though he were telling me a secret,

"I followed the truth in the Scriptures, God's Holy Word. When I had trouble understanding a particular verse in the Bible, I consulted my pastor, and he gave me the answer. I attended church each Sunday and went to prayer meetings twice a week. So, I know I did the right thing to get to heaven, but I still can't figure out how these others got here with their strange ways," said Joe.

His conceit put me off, but I couldn't help myself. I hoped I wasn't doing something to displease God when I asked,

"Joe, could it be possible that there is more than one way to heaven?"

"That's not what I was told, and I am a true believer. I don't know where you get these strange ideas. You don't know your Bible. The New Testament is full of truth as to how you get to heaven. It's all about believing in Jesus as the Son of God, His death upon the cross and the forgiveness of sins. You know, if you don't straighten out and accept the truth that the Bible teaches, you, too, will go to hell with the other unbelievers," replied Joe.

After this conversation I had to go on to ask others what they believed about how they arrived in heaven. Each was convinced that they had the answer. The orthodox Christians relied on the infallibility of the Bible. The Orthodox Jews referred to the Torah, the prophets and the Talmud as their basis for belief. The Muslims said that the Koran was their ultimate authority. The Church of Jesus Christ of Latter Day Saints used the Bible as well as The Book of Mormon.

Members of American Indian tribes could not understand what the other sections of the ISM group said. They had never heard of the Bible or the deliverance from hell – it was an idea that had never reached them. They had traditionally relied on their cultural and tribal customs such as sun worship and the belief in spirits for their vision of the nature of God and heaven. They believed fervently in their religious traditions handed down to them by the elderly sages among them.

The same was true of those people from other cultures. To my surprise, there were also Buddhists and those who believed in Hindu interpretations of life and death. How did these Asian faiths ever make it into God's heaven?

There had to be some mistake. But here they were. Could I have been wrong all these years in believing that God was quite exclusive in His choice for those who would enter heaven? I was taught that God only chose the elect as His small group to enter heaven. Was God really that inclusive, that He would permit in heaven such extreme groups, unfamiliar to most westerners? I doubted it. But I had to ask around, maybe check it out with the prophets and saints. They would have the answer.

As I said above, the only thing the ISMS members had in common was their notion that they had the only exclusive reservation to heaven. They universally attacked the other groups and judged them for having beliefs in systems other than their own. I heard members of one group say they knew that the devil had gotten into the heads and hearts of the others and had led them astray.

Some of the Christian fundamentalists in heaven described it as "spiritual warfare" instigated by the devil, Satan, in his contest with God for the hearts of humans. This conflicted directly with what I was told growing up. I did not expect that Satan would either be in heaven or have any influence there. On Earth, perhaps, but in heaven? They had to be wrong.

All this put me in a very confused state. Why were these various religious groups in heaven, and why were they all together? I decided to make a quick trip back to the OSAC to talk to some of the old prophets and saints. They must have the answer.

After some discussion, I got a clue, a hint at the answer. I received a report from one of Methuselah's assistants, a saint named Thomas, one of the New Testament apostles. He had the weather-worn, leathery face of a fisherman. His long flowing beard gave him the look of a sage; his demeanor spoke of authority.

With a voice of clarity and precision, cultivated from years in heaven answering the queries of new arrivals, Thomas said,

"These diverse religious groups have one thing in common. They all feel they have the exclusive answer to the existential questions on Earth. Here in heaven, they have one task. They are all guilty of one huge sin – that of judging and condemning others, for which Jesus railed against the Pharisees. That is their main problem. Their job in heaven is to become more understanding, more loving, more open and inclusive and to stop the arrogance of believing they have the sole corner on truth.

"People on Earth tend to think simplistically. They are very provincial. It's a holdover from tribal days. You know the thinking of primitive folks, 'Only our group should live. The strangers on the other side of the hill are our enemies and must be eradicated – before they kill us.' In modern times, humans were not as confined to small groups. Rather, it was one nation against another. The world has not yet evolved into a 'one world' concept, even at the present time.

"God's world and His universe are far too complicated for anything to be boiled down to one single view of things," continued Thomas. "The plan God had in mind, from eternity, was for all to come to Him, as they are all His creatures. God is merciful and His mercy endures forever. These folks will truly become citizens of heaven when they are able to include all the others who move among them and share their love forever. They have to give up their earthly ways of thinking and believing. They have to give up the idea that they are special, and that their religious convictions are the only way to heaven."

Wow! That changed everything. I was beginning to understand something of the magnitude of God's love and the immense nature of His compassion for the frailties of human nature. But I suspected that there was still an enormous amount to learn about God. I nurtured the hope that He would reveal more mysteries to me and others before long.

But how was all this to come about? How were all these folks in the "ISMS" going to learn how to be non-judgmental and loving to all? Well, I asked Thomas and he told me that God had a plan in mind. A few millennia ago, He held a meeting with the prophets and saints and got them in on the case. God explained it in His heavenly manner, but since Thomas could not remember every word verbatim, and there were no tape recorders in heaven, I had to make do with the following version. I didn't want to misquote God, so I got permission from those who attended the meeting to paraphrase Him.

Out of the clouds, God spoke with a holy, empathic voice along these lines.

"How could humankind ever conceive of me, their Creator, and of a heaven that would not include all the humans to whom I have given life? If I were still an Old Testament God, I would come down hard on them, and they would get a taste of my well-documented wrath. But as you know, I have changed, and I am now showing the merciful side of myself; I deal with things as exemplified by my Son, Jesus, who taught humans to love each other.

"I know what happened in the old days. I remember Noah and the flood. Those were bad times, and I have some regrets about allowing that to happen – destroying all but Noah and his family. I had hoped that the free will I gave to humans would result in many, if not all, coming to my ways of viewing things. But humankind was not mature enough to cope with that much free will. All the power that free will implied went to humankind's childlike notion that they were special.

"It was a child's dream, that only they would be saved. It's every young child's dream to be the only one loved by parents or, at least, to be the one loved best. They had the arrogance to literally say, 'To hell with everybody else.' You could call it a celestial mistake if you must, or the sinful pride of human beings.

"Regardless, in heaven, there is the opportunity to set it all straight, and that's what I am determined to do. Humans simply do not know how to give up their egos and live for the other person. Sometimes, on Earth, there were men and women who devoted their lives to others. It is not only those like St. Augustine, St. Francis, and in modern times, Gandhi, Dr. Schweitzer and Mother Teresa, but also the folks who are unknown and unheralded, who every day serve those in need. But the mass of humans focus on their own immediate concerns.

"So, as God, I have asked the prophets, saints, mullahs, and shamans to visit the ISMS group on a rotating basis and teach them the basics of my love and mercy. They have to give up their pride and judgmental natures. Many have been taught and have graduated to other groups – they no longer need the counseling of these leaders. But those still in the ISMS group have been a stiff-necked people, and they all seem glued to their particular view and are deaf to alternative ways of thinking.

"What pains me most, as their Creator, is that some of the isms on Earth claim their view of truth by quoting me for their belief. It would have been one thing to feel certain about a religious belief, but why did they all attribute their views of 'truth' to me?

"I know about the revealed truths that all these folks quote, but why don't they understand that one revelation of truth does not mean that all others are wrong? It was my plan to give the various civilizations the opportunity to understand things in their language and in their time. Without putting my revelations in the right context, humans would not have been able to comprehend the meaning of their existence at all. It was the only way that each could understand the nature of my creation and get to know me.

"For example, in biblical times, folks needed a God of judgment to help them differentiate good from evil, right from wrong. They needed the law, the commandments, the threat of judgment – Sheol – and the reward of heaven. Even with all my biblical revelations, many had no faith in my infinite grace. They defied me. Even the threat of punishment did not deter them from sin.

"In New Testament times, the apostles spread the word about the love of Jesus, which was a big improvement for the embattled tribes and cultures that existed then.

"Other civilizations, like Native Americans, who lived by the sun, stars and what the Earth provided, needed to have a faith in the celestial heavens as drawn up by their local shaman. Each culture had a chance to know me in a different way.

"It might help you to look at it this way. The various cultures and religions are like parts of a symphony. Each musician has learned his or her instrument from childhood, just as each person in a given group has learned his culture or religion well. The musician usually is not expert at any other instrument. A person from one culture does not readily understand another's background and beliefs, not without much study. Alone, each culture may work well by itself. But it takes the combined effort of all the cultures to make a civilization just as it takes all the instruments of a symphony to create beautiful music.

"I have allowed cultures to develop as parts of the earthly symphony that is mine. However, my symphony does not always play harmoniously. Too often there is a cacophony of noise coming from my world.

"In spite of the Savior's message, the world continued to show signs of war, selfishness and neglect of others. There have been Holy wars such as the Crusades, even wars among believers in Jesus – like the Catholics and Protestants fighting for years in Ireland.

"So, on Earth, there would never be a way to ever right the wrongs that occurred. Only in heaven can groups like the ISMS give up their arrogance and judgment. Only in heaven can peace be created so that all will live in harmony.

"Although I am the Creator and these are my people, sometimes I become annoyed at these groups of humans who are so stubborn and closed-minded. Next time, I'll do it differently, so I don't have to make so many corrections. When I created human beings on other planets, I did it in a way that avoided many of these pitfalls. Planet Earth has always been my biggest problem."

Well, this explanation from God certainly made sense, and I took it to heart and meditated on it for a long time. God is good. He is patient. He truly wants humans to live lives of love and devotion to others. His wish is that all come to Him, and only He can make that happen. There was a lot of information to absorb here. I put it in my memory bank for further digestion at a later date.

I took a deep breath and realized that what I had learned here need not be reported back to God, since He is the author of it all. I began to wonder if my role of ambassador to heaven had any use at all, but I continued to move around to the next group. If I am not needed to do this, I guess one of the saints will tell me.

"Prophet ill sustains his holy call
Who finds not heav'ns to suit the tastes of all."

Thomas Moore, *Lalla Rookh: The Veiled Prophet*

CHAPTER 6

I had to move on to another group and see what was happening there. I walked along, or to be more accurate, flew along, since I was now a spirit and had no feet to walk with, at least sometimes. Here in heaven, body and spirit constantly change. As a result, you don't always know what shape you're in.

On the other side of a hill – or possibility a cloud that resembled a hill – I noticed another exclusive group. It was called the PROPHESY ONLY CLUB (POC). I was dying to know who was in it. Dying? Here's an example of how you have to watch your verbs in heaven, since what applied on Earth does not work in heaven. Making this move to heaven is harder than I thought it would be. If it's not knowing whether you are a spirit or in body form, it's worrying about your language.

Anyway, as I approached this group, I noticed a stone tablet with names on it. Isaiah was first on the list. He was clearly in charge – the head honcho. Jeremiah, Ezekiel, Daniel and some of the lesser prophets were on the list – Amos, Jonah, Micah and others. For a moment, I was taken aback, when I saw the name

St. John, the Divine, but then I remembered that he had written the book of Revelation, which entitled him to be with the old-timers on the prophesy gig.

At the bottom of the list was a note in large black letters: MEMBERS ONLY. That was a bit intimidating, but I was informed that I might attend one of their meetings as an observer as long as I did not try to predict the future. I agreed since I had no interest in being a prophet. Also, I wanted to see if they were still engaged in foretelling coming events, or if it was no longer necessary. I decided to ask Isaiah about the group, since he was the leader. But as I approached him, he looked a bit distant, and I must say even unfriendly. He probably was becoming tired of newcomers with all their repetitive questions. I turned around and tried to find someone else.

Of all the prophets I remembered reading about on Earth, Daniel was the one I admired the most. I found him quietly talking to the others. He looked quite handsome, well proportioned and muscular, which made me wonder, for the moment, why physical stature was that important in heaven. I had the idea that physical concerns were strictly Earthbound concepts, and that heaven's spirit-filled atmosphere would eliminate physical attributes as important. But, again, I was surprised by heaven's failure to conform to my rigid planet Earth expectations.

I approached Daniel to ask my questions. He was not dressed in robes and sandals and did not look like an Old Testament prophet. He was wearing jeans, a tennis shirt and running shoes. Makes sense. I always thought of him as a sporty type, confronting lions and activities foreign to the other prophets. I wondered how he came up with that outfit, but then I remembered that those in heaven could be as old as they wanted and dress in any garb they preferred. Actually, he looked like one of my tennis buddies. I found that hard to put together, but heaven was full of amazing things.

"Daniel," I said, "it's a pleasure to meet you."

He was quick to reply, "I am pleased to meet you too. I understand that you have been given a special role in heaven as God's ambassador. If there is anything I can do to help you with your job, be sure to call on me."

"Well, Daniel, I can begin right now. There are some questions that have troubled me on Earth, and, so far, I have not found the answers to my queries. As a child, when I read about you in the Bible, I always saw you as a model to emulate. And now that I see you here, perhaps you can shed some light on what has been bothering me for some time. My question is, why was it necessary that prophesies be made and fulfilled? Also, are you and the others still engaged in prophesy?"

Daniel seemed, at first, to think my questions were naïve. But he quickly realized that I had only recently come from Earth and did not have the benefit of familiarity with general information available on heaven's version of the Internet, to which anyone here in heaven could gain access. I learned later that to reach this virtual media, one did not have to "log on." All you had to do was "Google" subjects in your mind and the results would immediately come to your awareness. Pretty neat, don't you think? And this mental computer never crashes.

Of course, there is no substitute for direct communication with the leaders in heaven. I felt I needed firsthand direct contact. So I left the Googling for later.

Daniel talked in a soft but resonant voice.

"My son, God was all too familiar with the true nature of man ever since the fall of Adam and Eve. God saw the repeated turn to idol worship and the continual backsliding of his people, the Israelites.

"After the great flood and Noah's survival, the population grew large. God watched the building of the Tower of Babel, which was initially designed by the people for the worship of

God. As the building of this enormous structure progressed, the people agreed that it was a way to keep the inhabitants together and dedicated it to themselves rather than God.

"There was only one language at the time, according to Genesis, and God, being displeased by the builders' change of mind, decided to confuse their 'tongues' and create many different languages. In so doing, God caused the people to scatter throughout the land.

"Even after He destroyed the world with the flood, the people continued to sin; God's chosen people often doubted what they were told, so He called upon the prophets to tell those on Earth what was to happen in the future. He brought Isaiah, Ezekiel and the others to warn the folks about their sin and tell them about futuristic events in the years ahead. They also prophesied about the coming of the Messiah and told of visions of heaven.

"It was God's eternal hope that humankind would be encouraged to believe in what they were told and then obey His commandments. In spite of all of this, doubt remained, and only some of God's people continued to worship Him."

"I understand that so far," I said, "but why couldn't God inspire more people to believe? Why is the Bible filled with more sinful behavior than good works? Even David, who the Bible tells us was a man after God's own heart, appeared to be one of the most extravagant sinners of all time. He did some drastic things like arranging the killing of Uriah so that he could get his hands on Uriah's wife. How evil can you get?"

Daniel looked up to the clouds as though he was not getting my question. Then he smiled and said, "You must realize that one sin is as bad as the other in the sight of God. No sin is acceptable. Yet, God wanted humans to serve and obey Him without coercion – to do it on their own. He created free will for humans to do good or evil, so that all could show Him glory by obedience and praise. And I hope you remember how David repented of his sin and pleaded for God's forgiveness as recorded in the 51st Psalm in the Bible."

At that moment I had a thought that troubled me. It was possibly heretical. But I was asking the big questions, so I felt I had to do it.

I confronted Daniel with the most puzzling of all mysteries about heaven.

"Daniel, perhaps you can tell me. There are those who have been exposed to various faiths and have not acknowledged God as the Creator. Some are agnostic, and others are atheists. They take the scientific approach and need everything proven to them in logical terms. They seem to be unable to reach into their souls and get a faith perspective. What about them? In spite of revealed truth, they don't acknowledge God at all and think that this mystery which is planet Earth will soon end, and we will all become dust again and that will be the end of it all. What does God do with these obstinate individuals?"

By this time, Daniel realized that he was not talking to someone who had not thought about these matters a great deal. The old prophet looked at me with a kind, empathetic smile and said,

"My son, all the mysteries of the universe are not revealed to us. We simply do not have all the answers. When I first arrived in heaven, I was also puzzled by this same question. I asked some of the older prophets about it. To my surprise, they didn't have the answer either. They could only say that God's ways are inscrutable. But they assured me that as heavenly time went on, we would all become more knowledgeable about these enigmas."

Then I asked the other question that troubled me. "What about the young children who died in infancy, or who were aborted or miscarried before birth? What will happen to them?"

"God in His mercy has no limits," said Daniel. "His love is

endless. If He chooses, He is able to save anyone, even those from many religious backgrounds. I believe He will also save the young children. But the absolute truth on this issue has not been revealed to us fully. Although we do not have all the answers, much is clearer here in heaven than when we were on Earth. As I just said, things will become less puzzling in the future."

*****

After that informative talk with Daniel, I reflected on what this PROPHESY ONLY group was going to do with all the time they had on their spiritual hands. After all, there was no more necessity for telling the future. It seemed like they had succumbed to history, had outlived their usefulness and had an outmoded and irrelevant role.

So I checked with Daniel and he said, "It may look like we have nothing to do, but you must realize that in the old days, we did more than sit around all day and speak about the future. We were teachers, preachers and priests to the people.

"Here in heaven, we do the same thing. I understand that you will be visiting with all the groups here. Unless you have already visited clubs like the doctors' or lawyers' groups, you have no idea how much help is needed to get these groups straightened out and acceptable to God. And have you seen the ISMS group yet? Talk about problems. They have them in numbers that rival the galaxies.

"Many of the groups have a lot of issues to resolve before they can be presented to God as whole and worthy of being here. God is good and forgives all, but some of these guys are the hardest to please. You'll see what I mean when you call on them."

I stepped back and reflected on what I had heard. Some of my best friends on Earth were doctors and lawyers and belonged to the other groups. I wondered what Daniel had in mind. I thought I would check into the lawyer group next, but as I moved about,

I saw something that alerted me: a sign about politics. What? Politics in heaven? I had to move closer.

Oh, one more thing before I leave this group. You may be wondering why Daniel was not in the OLD SOULS' AUTHORITATIVE CLUB. As it turns out, anyone in heaven may belong to a number of groups and is not confined to being a member of only one club. So expect to see the heavenly cast in any number of places.

**"If there is one part of the Christian
message that people have rejected with
incomparable obstinacy, it is faith in
the equal worth of all souls and races
before the Father who is in heaven."**

Francois Muriac, *Life of Jesus*

CHAPTER 7

On my way to what was clearly the most active club in
heaven, the lawyers' group, I suddenly realize that I have not
filled you in on what is happening with God and his son, Jesus. I
don't know about you, but while on Earth, I was always puzzled
by a lot of things I heard about the life of Jesus, such as the
virgin birth, the miracles, the resurrection and the other things
that can be read in the Christian creeds.

For example, the Apostles' Creed states that Jesus ascended
into heaven and is sitting at the right hand of God the Father.

I always have trouble visualizing God having a right hand,
although the Bible also says that man was created in God's own
image. Elsewhere in the Bible, He is said to exist as a Spirit. In
writing about Him, we humans always seem more comfortable
putting Him in human form – anthropomorphizing the picture.
We do this with lots of things when we use metaphors.

But when it comes to God, I just can't see Him with a right
hand, although in the world of art, God is often given a human

form. For example, I do appreciate it when I view Michelangelo's *Creation of Adam,* painted on the ceiling of the Sistine Chapel, where God appears in physical form with an extended hand.

When we say in earthly terms that someone is his "right hand man" or he is "my right arm," we mean that that person is very important to the functioning of the individual in charge. So, it would not surprise you if I found Jesus to be central to God's plan in heaven. But, like others in heaven, Jesus can appear as a spirit or in His resurrected body.

If Jesus is not physically sitting at God's right hand all day, just what is he doing as the pivotal manager of God's plan? Of course, I don't really know, but in my dream He was quite busy.

As I went around heaven to the various groups, I came upon Jesus frequently. He often appeared in glowing attire, but also in unexpected clothes. His garments were a mixture of all the many clothes worn by the earthly cultures that were represented in heaven.

At one time in these different guises, Jesus could have passed for a trial lawyer in a three-piece suit and vest. At another time, He looked like a South American Indian with His colorful garments. One day, I saw Him in casual clothes talking to the orthodox Christians; another time He was dressed like an orthodox Jew with black hat and clothes, hair in curls, talking with the rabbis. Next, I saw Him dressed like an Islamic sheik going to a mosque for daily prayers. At another time He looked more like a cave man, dressed only in a loin cloth and carrying a wooden club. Can you imagine that? Well, I got the impression that in this outfit He was helping the prehistoric groups that were in heaven.

His constant changes astonished me. I imagined Him having a heavenly valet to help him with His extensive wardrobe. I began to wonder why Jesus did not appear like we always imagined Him in an earthly form. Why did He have to continually change

His outfits to conform to the tastes of the groups He was visiting?

Let me ask you. On Earth, what was your image of Jesus? From Sunday school pictures I remember, He often had blue eyes and long, light hair and wore a robe and sandals. In reality, Jesus could not possibly have had light hair and blue eyes, but some artists in our culture often made it so. In heaven, Jesus dressed to fit into the group He was visiting. If He appeared in a different guise than the groups were accustomed to, He would have been looked at with suspicion.

So, at least for a while, Jesus had to look like the groups to which He was ministering. God's hope was that in the future all heaven's inhabitants would not judge Jesus simply by what He was wearing. I concluded from this that earthly defenses die hard. It takes a long time to free humans from judging others by their appearances – maybe an eternity.

What was the role of Jesus in heaven? On one occasion I had the privilege of seeing Him up close in one of the groups. It wasn't easy to obtain an audience with Him, but after some effort in contacting His staff, I was successful in talking with Him for a few minutes. I was thrilled to be able to do this, as I personally knew no one who had ever talked to Him. Later I found out that Jesus talked to many people here in heaven.

With eager anticipation mixed with some trepidation, I approached Him and asked my questions. He was very gentle and spoke with a soft, mellow voice, unlike any I had ever heard before. He had beautiful dark hair, brown eyes and a radiant face. He looked at me in the most kindly manner as I settled in to ask Him what was on my mind.

"Jesus," I said, "thank you for seeing me. From what I have observed, you are extremely busy here in heaven. My conception of life after death was quite different, as I had expected to be quiet, sing praises to God and have the eternal rest so often spoken of on Earth. Yet here I find a great deal of activity, and even You are really busy. Obviously, You are not just sitting at the right hand of God enjoying your privileged place." I had to refrain from an audible chuckle when I said that.

"Why is it necessary for you to go around to all the groups and talk to them continuously?"

Jesus smiled at that remark and said, "You are right. There is little leisure here in heaven, except, perhaps, in the Old Soul's Group. They deserve rest for all they have done on Earth as well as in heaven. And even here, people do age somewhat. It's not that they look that much older. They just do less, and of course, they never die. God promised eternal life and that's what occurs here."

Jesus continued, "But let me get to your question. Contrary to what many folks on Earth think, life here in heaven is not being grafted to a cloud and singing hymns to God all day long. That is not what would please God, our Father. He wants the inhabitants here to become peaceful, calm, non-judgmental and live with others in a loving manner.

"I tried to convey this during my brief stay on Earth, when I said that folks on Earth should love God and love their neighbor as themselves. That was not an easy thing to do, because of the selfish nature of human beings. As you know, when they die and leave their earthly ways and come here, no human being is fully developed. They are not yet completely redeemed and transformed to God's expectation.

"On Earth, many think that accepting God and trying to live the good life is all that is required to please God. But no one on Earth does this in a perfect way. Redemption on Earth means that we are forgiven for our transgressions, but it does not mean we have arrived at perfection. It takes heaven to do that! So what is begun on Earth in the religious life is completed in heaven. Here is where redemption and salvation finally occurs.

"What is my job? It is to do the Father's will and bring

everyone to the redeemed and perfect state. That takes time and a lot of work, since many of the folks who die and come here are in a pathetic, albeit quite human, condition. But these are the very folks that I tried to reach while on Earth. Even in heaven, people become discouraged and tend to give up their desire to arrive at perfection. No one ever said that heaven would be an eternal feast. But I am here to assist those in the various groups to reach the ideal of perfection. That is my Father's will."

The explanation that Jesus gave was interesting to me, and I wasn't really surprised, as I had been told by the prophets and saints here that heaven was much like Jesus described. So I put these ideas into my spiritual tote bag.

But before leaving Jesus, I thought of another question to ask Him. I know how he railed against the Pharisees in His time on Earth. He despised their tendency to judge others and live by the letter of the law, missing the mark on its spirit. I asked Jesus if this was the most important thing that folks on Earth should be aware of as the foundation of his teaching.

"Son, you are correct. The Pharisees were hypocrites, and this sin is very prevalent among many folks on Earth, especially among those who profess a faith in God.

"That was one of the things I tried to teach those I saw on Earth, but the more basic teaching had to do with love – not just ordinary love between family members and friends. The love I tried to get people to understand went far beyond traditional ideas of love. Remember what I said about loving your enemies and praying for those who persecute you. That takes real love. To understand, believe and act as though all humans are God's children, regardless of how bad their behavior might be. That takes love, which can only be given to folks by the grace of God. Most human beings, on their own, do not love in this manner. They are often selfish, defensive of their own behavior and prone to do what immediately benefits them.

"I know how hard it is to love others. It is such a natural tendency to look out for oneself. That is the basic nature of the child, and it is necessary to grow up and become an adult. But the mature child of God, as he or she develops, must strive to go far beyond this narcissistic state. I taught that God's creatures must learn to love others as they would want to be loved by others. It is an earthly goal that I have taught. Although many humans attain a considerable degree of love, only in heaven is love fully and completely realized. Only then will God be able to say that He is 'well pleased' with His creatures."

Ah! What a time I had, talking with Jesus. As you can imagine, I was very happy and excited to do so. I thanked Him profusely and went on my way. As I left, I was aware of a profound sense of ease and contentment and a wonderful reflective mood that I assumed came from being in the presence of Jesus. Never on Earth had I had such a pervasively peaceful feeling. All was right in God's heaven. I just hoped that everyone there could experience that same kind of rapture.

Meeting Jesus! What a thrill! If nothing else happened in heaven after this, I would be very content.

"A teacher who arouses a feeling in us for one good action, one good poem, accomplishes more than the teacher who fills our heads with interminable lists of natural objects."

Goethe, Elective Affinities

CHAPTER 8

As I left Jesus, I thought about what he had said about most of the folks in heaven, all working on some kind of self-improvement.

It occurred to me that some human beings must have lived very fulfilling lives on Earth and perhaps needed little coaching in heaven toward getting to a more perfect state. There must be some persons who managed to reach the near-perfect goal on Earth. I am thinking of the prophets and saints as examples of such fulfillment: Abraham, Isaac, Jacob, Job, to mention just a few. St. Augustine, St. Thomas Aquinas, St. Teresa and Dr. Schweitzer are others who lived full spiritual lives.

Thoughts of people I have known come to mind. I can think of some folks who died prematurely and thus had little time to reach the goal of spiritual fulfillment. Others have not realized such goals even though they lived to become aged. And then there are the many individuals who appear to have no taste for anything as vague as religion. If I were to talk with them about sports, how to make money or the next vacation they are planning, they would be fully involved. But mention anything that smacks of religion, and they grow silent. Their interests revolve around immediate realities, not spiritual or existential concerns.

While thinking about this issue, I suddenly saw at a distance a woman who looked amazingly like my fourth grade teacher. Approaching the woman, I saw that it was her, Ann Bouma Morris. Wow! I knew she would be here, but I was not certain what she would be doing or in what corner of heaven she would be. If anyone deserved to be here it was Ann. Her earthly life had been filled with exemplary Christ-like deeds, and I was privileged to follow her journey on Earth until she died at age eighty-five.

I greeted her with open arms. We embraced warmly. I was so excited to see her. It brought back all of the glow and radiance of our earthly meetings. I felt like talking to her for hours. But to my surprise, in thoughts that followed, my high school social studies teacher, Cornelius Bontekoe, also came to mind. As I was talking to Ann, he suddenly appeared. He was here too. On Earth we had never embraced. Real men did not do that in my stern Dutch culture. But here we recognized what on Earth had been a close bond. I hugged him with feelings of gratitude for what he had done in my life. What an exhilarating experience – to have both of my best teachers on Earth meet me here in heaven.

The two of them were close friends on Earth and here in heaven that bond continued. My surprise at seeing my favorite teachers, both of whom influenced me greatly on Earth, was overwhelming. These two individuals lived very different but very fulfilling lives in their time. I could not think of many ways in which the heavenly atmosphere could improve on them. Both were highly unusual characters. I have to tell you about them by reflecting on my early school days.

*****

My first three grades in elementary school, hardly stellar memories, were taught by strict teachers, stereotypes of rigid, humorless old maids, although they were not old chronologically.

My first grade teacher yelled at me for not being able to trace a "J" on the blackboard with sufficient accuracy. I remember being very upset and shedding a few tears about my inadequacy and shame; I was easily intimidated.

On another occasion she embarrassed me by calling in the second grade teacher to show her my disgraceful behavior.

The teacher (I am not surprised that I can't remember her name) had a rule in the classroom that students were to sit up straight in the chairs at our desks. It was forbidden to sit on one leg, even though this position, at times, was more comfortable for me.

Occasionally, I forgot this prohibition and sat with one leg tucked under the other. My trousers were the old fashioned "knickers" that had a metal buckle below each knee. When I sat on one leg the metal did a job on the seat. Over time there were many scratches on the seat; about these I was unaware.

When my teacher discovered the damage to the finish on the seat, she accused me of scratching the seat with my finger nails. I did not deny this. Her imagination of my scratching trumped my fear of violating the prohibition of leg sitting. I was told to stay after school, at which time the second grade teacher was called in to witness my aberrant behavior.

My feelings of shame were a typical childhood reaction to discipline. (Don't acknowledge what you actually did wrong – disobey the rule about leg sitting, but take responsibility for what it was assumed you did. All that horrible finger scratching actually seemed to me like a lesser infraction). I was very embarrassed, and left school that day in a funk.

The third grade was equally uninspiring. Nothing of note

happed that was traumatic, but after completing the third grade, I had a distinct dislike for early education. If this trend had continued, I could have been a failed dropout after eighth grade.

But a wonderful series of events occurred. I entered my fourth grade class to a delightful new teacher. She was a young, blue-eyed blonde, a smiling woman known to us affectionately as Miss Bouma. She made you want to learn the required reading, writing and math skills, but more that that, she made you feel important and special to her as an individual. Many years later, in a letter, she remembered me as always smiling and happy. This was clearly a reaction to her sparkling personality, which elicited the expression of that side of my persona. In high school, another teacher described me as the "great stone face." What a contrast!

Miss Bouma lifted my spirits and encouraged learning as no other teacher had done before.

Our teacher thought it was part of her job to play with us after school, especially in winter, when we all went sledding and ice skating together. In today's climate of political correctness, some parents would suspect the teacher's motives in spending so much time with her students after school hours. But that was another time, when child abuse was not a major societal concern.

Annette "Ann" Bouma came from the same Calvinist, Dutch immigrant background as her students. Her father was a pastor in a conservative Christian Reformed Church. She was made of strong, independent stuff, clearly out of a different mold from the rest of us. We loved and adored her. I saw her again in high school, although I did not have her as a teacher. I would come to see her yet again much later, when I was in college and in a variety of other situations.

After this amazing year in fourth grade, I had an ambivalent feeling about the remaining teachers in elementary school. Mostly, the teachers were well-meaning but uninspiring.

It was the early 1940s – the beginning of World War II. Many young men were drafted into the military or volunteered to fight for their country. A few women volunteered for the Army (WACS) or the Navy (WAVES). I knew of only one such person – my fourth grade teacher. She entered the Army and rose to the rank of Captain.

While she was serving our country, Miss Bouma met and married an architect and artist named Dick Morris. Much later I learned that Dick had a background that included Afro-American, Native American and Irish roots. At the time, I had no idea of his ancestry. He had no physical attributes that suggested his genetic roots other than perhaps Irish ancestry. The conservative, provincial parents of Ann Bouma, however, did not look favorably on her marriage to this man. They, like many conservative folks of the time, considered this romance a "mixed marriage." In retrospect this was hardly in keeping with the teaching of Jesus, who freely interacted with many social outcasts whom He met during His time on Earth. Somehow the teachings of Jesus failed to overcome the basic prejudices of the day.

What happened next was a series of events in the lives of Ann and Dick Morris that was dramatically different from the way any of Ann's colleagues or friends lived. Their plans and actions preceded the popular fringe cultures of the sixties by about two decades.

The newly married couple purchased seven acres of land in a rural setting in New Jersey, now a built-up suburb. They set up a tent on the property in early summer and lived in it until November, as they proceeded to build a house. Never one to shirk from manual labor, Ann pitched in to help, even while pregnant with her first child. By late fall of that year, they had a roof over their heads.

The home was made of cinder blocks and had heating pipes

that ran under the cement floors, an uncommon method of providing heat at the time. They painted the interior of the house themselves and had drapes made of burlap bags hung on the windows. Some of Dick's paintings were on the walls. I knew of no other home that in any way resembled the uniqueness of the Morris home. They admired the modern architecture of Frank Lloyd Wright, and in some ways tried to emulate him in building their house.

The adjoining property was a place for goats and chickens to roam around. Goats' milk, chickens, eggs, fruits and vegetables from their garden made up the Morris family's attempt to have a self-sustaining existence – "organic farming" long before the fad had become commercialized.

My knowledge of all of this is not from hearsay. These were people who welcomed the visits of young adults they knew at any time. It was not unusual for my future wife, Marge, and I to visit with them on a Saturday night with little or no notice.

One summer, before we were married, Ann and Dick asked me to house-sit their home for a week, while they went away. This was a huge thrill for me as they allowed me the privilege of driving their old Army jeep during the time that they were gone. (I had no car of my own.) Part of the reason for having me there was to feed and care for their chickens and goats.

Feeding the chickens was a familiar task, since my father had a small chicken farm on our next-door lot. But milking the goats was not something my childhood had prepared me for. It was only with great patience and determination that I was able to extract milk from those stubborn animals.

At this early date the word "hippie" was not yet generally heard. To me the Morris family was one of the prototypes of the later hippie generation in terms of their lifestyle. But, they had a distinctly Christian approach to everything that they did. They lived simply, and in their daily lives they showed an unselfish, loving and caring spirit so often preached in my religious community but not always practiced.

Here is one example. It was 1950. No strangers to the big city nearby, Ann and Dick took Marge and me to a Japanese restaurant in New York, perhaps the first such Japanese dining establishment in the city after the war. To us it was so unusual, as we were young and unaccustomed to dining out, especially in New York. The restaurant was in Midtown. I remember climbing a flight of stairs to get to the dining area. The menu was strange to us, but Ann and Dick made us comfortable with their familiarity with the choices. More important than the food was the congeniality of being around these wonderful people.

The Morris family had seven children. With the self-confidence Ann and Dick possessed, they decided to homeschool their children. At the time, I knew of no one else who was trying to educate their own children. Only years later did this become a more common phenomenon.

Having no precedent in the town of Mahwah or even in New Jersey, Ann had to fight for the privilege of homeschooling by taking the case to court in their town. She contended that she was a certified school teacher and thus was able to provide an adequate or better education for her children. She won the case, and all went well in the Morris household until the children reached their early teenage years. They wanted the social contacts that traditional school provided, so they discontinued homeschooling and finished their high school education by attending Eastern Academy, our local Christian School, where Dick was an art teacher.

The Morris family then embarked on another new and as of yet untried experiment. They bought a farm in Stillwater, in rural western New Jersey. Having both been teachers, Dick and Ann saw the need for a special school for children with learning and emotional problems. This was long before Child Study Teams in public schools or the diagnosis of learning disabilities and teaching techniques to help correct these learning problems.

In time, "The School of the Arts" enrolled forty students. The students were given a broad education which included a wide variety of the arts and yoga instruction along with Christian principles. The students were taken on many field trips to places as far away as the Franklin Institute in Philadelphia, Kentucky and Appalachia. Marge and I visited the school and were quite impressed with the uniqueness of what the Morris family was doing.

But just as their dream of a fresh approach to education was being fulfilled, tragedy struck. While traveling in New Hampshire with his son Darvil, Dick Morris was killed, and his son was severely injured. The sudden loss of her husband was devastating to Ann and her plans for the school were in jeopardy. They had always struggled with financial concerns at the school. Then, without any warning, an arsonist set fire to the school building. After these setbacks, Ann was forced to close the school and reassess what to do with her life.

Following these horrible events, Ann obtained a job at Berea College in Kentucky, where she was an administrator and founder of Our Selves to Educate, a homeschooling resource. With considerable effort, she was able to recoup from her monumental losses – those of her husband and her dream school.

After she regained her stability and strength, she felt it was her calling to move to Harlem in New York City, where she worked with drug addicts and the homeless.

It was at this time, in 1980, on my birthday, which was curiously the same day as hers, that I received a letter from her. In it she said,

"I'm now 65, and ready to start Life II. In fact, it is in the birthing stage, and God and I are working on plans for the new life to be built on the old, yet distinct from it."

Her letter to me was prompted by what she had read in the newspaper about my wife, Marge, being elected to the U.S. Congress. She felt compelled to say how society and government policies differed from the teachings of Christ. She was particularly upset by the restraints on personal freedom and individual privacy and the lack of governmental concern for the poor, the minorities and the homeless. She feared that the new Moral Majority's efforts would infringe on the freedoms of citizens.

I answered her concerns explaining what Marge was attempting to do in the U.S. Congress. I especially noted Marge's work on the Hunger Committee and her trip to Ethiopia. Marge was the main force behind the Child Support Bill and the Family and Medical Leave Act. I told Ann we shared her concerns about the Moral Majority and that Marge was not part of that movement.

A few years later, in a delayed response to my letter, she wrote a long commentary on society, the government and the lack of attention to the words of Christ. She was quite adamant and angry about the failure of Christians to heed Christ's admonition to help "the poor, the sick, the imprisoned, and the naked." She despised moderation, and attempted to be the radical that resembled Jesus' ministry on Earth. She was not just talking the talk, but also walking the walk – fully. She was teaching biology, math and science at Malcolm King College in New York, and she had a monthly radio program to encourage seniors to become Elders in the community.

In her letter she said,

"I live very simply, my office= my home, a one-room apartment in central Harlem. Even though I come home often at night, and walk among junkies, drunks, prostitutes and derelicts, and ride the subways, I have never been even threatened. Time and again I have beheld legions of angels hovering in the streets, and God explains He is much more comfortable here than downtown where they refuse Christ's injunction – 'Go sell all that you have, give to the poor, and follow me.'"

My old fourth grade teacher went on to say that I should "forget the person you knew as Miss Bouma... I did not mean to hurt [by her criticism of Marge's work in the Congress], but goad you into a re-evaluation of our lives in that comfortable community in relation to God's counsel to do justly, to love mercy and walk humbly with God. It's not happening when we are 'at ease in Zion.' We are not meant to be comfortable: too much compensation demanded for past injustices."

It was quite a letter and a severe admonition. Very few people I know could have this kind of devotion to the poor and needy. I could only admire her Christ-like involvement in her work with the poorest and homeless of city life. At the same time, I could not imagine myself doing the same work. She was made of tougher stuff than I.

After thinking it through and perhaps rationalizing it, I concluded that we each have to make our peace with God and do what is within our talents and abilities. I take only small comfort in St. Paul's counsel, (Eph. 4:11) "And he gave some, apostles; and some, prophets; and some, evangelists and some, pastors and teachers." A similar verse in 1 Corinthians 12:28 says, "And God hath set some in the church, first apostles, secondarily prophets, thirdly teachers, after that miracles, then gifts of healings, helps, governments, diversities of tongues."

So, in the words of St. Paul, there are other things that one can do in the religious life, all of which makes up the entire body of the church.

Everyone cannot become as Christ-like as my fourth grade teacher. She was indeed unique. In my dream of heaven, I imagined that she was one of those rare creatures who would need very little assistance in heaven to become perfect in the sight of God. She had gone a long way on Earth toward the perfecting of her soul. In heaven she could well be a counselor or teacher to those who needed help.

I saw the life of my former teacher in marked contrast to the folks that were in the Exclusive ISMS Club. She had a firm faith and a strong determination to go her own way and tread her path as a devoted follower of Christ.

*****

I want to tell you about a second teacher, one who affected me immensely in high school. My interest in academics lagged there in deference to sports, until I entered the ninth grade at Eastern Academy. That sounds like an elite private school, but it was hardly elite.

The Dutch immigrants of the early twentieth century felt, as a group, that they should be "in this world but not of this world." They did not believe that their children would receive the proper biblical and religious foundation in public schools that was necessary to the Christian life. So they started their own Christian schools.

Families that could not afford the low cost of tuition were provided the funds through their churches. Teachers' salaries were far below the standard in public education. It was a bare-bones operation with dedicated teachers, committed to giving us Christian values along with academics. Bible study was a basic; the teaching of Reformed doctrine was considered essential. We were, in essence, the spiritual children of John Calvin. Our college in Grand Rapids, Michigan is called Calvin College.

In this small school environment, I was fortunate to encounter an intellectually provocative and caring social studies teacher and basketball coach named Cornelius Bontekoe.

By anyone's standards, "Bonte" did not attract us by his outward appearance. He was not particularly handsome or graced with any attractive exterior features. He had the looks of an everyman. He was cursed with a persistent stutter, which would have prevented any lesser man from being a high school teacher. But somehow, no student ever dared to mock or imitate him or even talk about his verbal deficit.

By his gentle provocation, he encouraged my interest in reading and critical thinking. In so doing, he encouraged me to touch on an area that I had not thought about, nor acquired from any family member – as none of them, except one brother, had had any education beyond elementary school.

Mr. Bontekoe required us to read selections about history from the author Charles Beard. He told us about the *Atlantic Monthly*, a magazine I had never heard of before. He taught us intellectual discernment in the area of politics. He made it clear that in any state or national election, the independents, rather than the political parties, basically controlled the outcome of the election. This was a concept that none of us had ever encountered before.

In one memorable moment he taught us about race relations. Some of our classmates had to come to school by bus from the neighboring towns of Paterson, Passaic and Clifton. In their daily commuting, they often were on the bus with African-Americans. When our teacher asked these mostly Dutch students what they thought of these citizens who differed from them, one of the kids in that class had the effrontery to say that "negroes smell."

The class was momentarily taken back until our teacher said in a loud and angry voice with disdain on his face,

"D-D-D-Dutchmen s-s-smell too!"

That astounded us, and we never forgot it. To this day, I become emotional just thinking about this incident. What a treasure our teacher "Bonte" was!

In one declarative, stuttering sentence, he set in motion the beginning of our education on the essence of prejudice. Any dissertation on race relations would probably have left us unmoved. Mr. Bontekoe was truly a legend in our school. Many students who had never given a thought to higher education were inspired to go to college through his teaching.

Later, after having graduated from medical school, I went back to see him.

He had become the principal of the high school. I asked him why he had given up teaching for administration. He said that he wanted to influence a "larger piece of the pie." I expressed my appreciation for all he had done to help inspire me toward my advanced education.

Shortly thereafter, at a relatively early age, "Bonte" suddenly died. His memory lives on in the lives of all who had contact with him. In retrospect, he had a short but complete life. He fulfilled his dreams. I saw his life in stark contrast to those members of the political group here in heaven, who I will describe next. These folks were always arguing with others about their beliefs as to what was the "right" way to think about any political issue.

Most of us have teachers, mentors or other idealized figures in our background, some of whom have had a marked influence on our lives, both positive and negative. I have often wondered what my life would have been like had I not been fortunate enough to encounter my two sainted school teachers, both of whom lived very fulfilling lives.

After the above diversion concerning my earthly life and the two wonderful teachers that inspired me, I realized that I was still in heaven. So, I took a deep breath of celestial air and gave some thought about where to go next. There was so much to do, but here in heaven, time was no issue; I had until eternity.

**"There is a holy mistaken zeal in politics
As well as in religion. By persuading others,
We convince ourselves."**

William Draper

CHAPTER 9

As I spirited my way about, I was truly shocked by what I saw – large signs: POLITICAL PARTIES ONLY, ALL OTHERS KEEP OUT, UNLESS YOU HAVE SOMETHING TO CONRIBUTE.

Why in heaven's name would there have to be political groups here? I thought that politics and political parties were just for us earthlings. But there they were, HEAVENLY LEADERS ONLY (HLS). Who were these elitist politicians absolutely convinced that they had the truth on what was best for governing the masses here in heaven?

One section in this group was THE ALMOST PERSUADED DOUBTERS (APD) section. These folks could not belong to any political party because they could never take a stand on either side of the political fence. Some members of this group had been political independents on Earth. They were above it all – above the daily grind of party politics.

I remember those people in my political associations on Earth. They were proud of their independent stand. Some were even snobbish about it. They let others do the grunt work of selecting the candidates for the various offices, whether on a local, state or national level. The independents often felt they were above the process of going about mingling with the masses, belonging to one political party or another.

But I noticed that these same independents were among the first to complain about the poor qualities of those running for office, those who had been selected in the primary voting process. I remember such comments as, "Why can't the Republicans (or Democrats) get someone who is smarter, more articulate or experienced than that guy?" Those folks that call themselves independents never seemed to take on the responsibility of candidate selection.

Since the area I was now in was political, I figured I would see the people who filled our history books, such as Washington, Jefferson or Lincoln as well as some modern day politicos like FDR, Truman, JFK, Ike and Reagan. But I found out that many historical figures had not been interested in joining the political group. I had to ask about that.

I saw someone who looked familiar, but I could not remember who he was. Nor did I want to ask. As God's ambassador, I didn't want to reveal my ignorance. And then I had a thought: isn't it amazing, that even here in heaven, I am still concerned about my ego and wish to appear knowledgeable. I guess it will take a while for that to disappear.

Just then, I saw a woman who looked like she might be able to answer some of my questions. She appeared quite trim in her blue blazer, red blouse, tan slacks and long flowing hair. As you may have noted, everyone here does not prefer to wear robes and sandals. Besides, politicians that I have known have never been dressed that way, except when they were on a paid vacation to an island where some lobbyist was trying to gain favors regarding legislation on a state or federal level. I walked up to this sharp-looking woman and posed my questions.

"Excuse me miss, could you answer a few questions about these political groups?" She seemed agreeable, quite friendly, and I must add, quite attractive with her winning smile. She told me her name was Nancy. I went on to ask my questions. She said she would be glad to try to answer.

"Thank you for your time, Nancy. To begin with, why do you need political clubs in heaven? After all, there is no government – local, state or federal. So, what is there to be organized about?"

"I suppose you haven't been in heaven long," she said. "You have to realize that when politicians come here, they are not in their fully realized state. They still think they have to change things. It's in their blood, in their DNA. They can't just stop thinking like politicians. They have to have agendas with things to change, elect people to office, do battle with opposing views and make various demands.

"Some want more freedom, others more restrictions and laws to contain aberrant behavior. Yes, once in a while there are those upstarts that want to start a movement or even a revolt, although, of course, the latter is not possible in heaven. Still others want rule by oligarchy despising democracy. So you can imagine there is much controversy. Sometimes you can't hear your own thoughts because of the volume of argument. Maybe we need a dictator to calm things down. These groups should not surprise you, as most of them are lawyers. With such a single-minded focus on things, they simply had to join the political group."

"I think I can understand that." I said. "It is hard to change what was so much a part of your life. But why aren't the famous figures of American history here? I thought I would find them in charge of some of the parties in this diverse group."

My host was a bit puzzled by my inquiry, but she was indulgent and said,

"The famous people in your history books are way beyond

the average politician as to individual growth toward their maturity. For example, Abraham Lincoln came from a poor rural setting and suffered many political defeats. Yet he became president of the country. That alone did not constitute a fulfilled life. He endured mental depression and the loss of several children, but somehow he was able to prevail and perform well as president. He was in charge during a very important part of the history of the United States, when civil war was raging. His determination to see the war through and set free the slaves was a remarkable feat of history. Although he was gunned down and killed prematurely, he nonetheless lived a very complete life and has gone down in history as having lived fully.

"Your president Roosevelt is another example. With worldwide depression and bread lines, he was able to begin the recovery from the economic devastation, while fighting the international horror of the rise of Hitler, the axis powers and Japan. Although he did not live to see the end of the war, his life was very full and complete. Such leaders have nothing to prove. They are not preoccupied with changing everything. They lived rather fulfilled lives on Earth, and their work was finished, except for perfecting their spirits to conform to heaven's ultimate goal.

"Many of the other politicos from Earth have such egos and they act as though God can't take care of things here and needs them to alter conditions. They feel constrained to always change things, even though nothing needs changing. It's such a habit."

I offered, "Knowing a bit about how political types think, I can understand their reluctance to give up this way of life. But how long will this take? Some of these folks are quite intransigent, as I remember."

"Yes," Nancy said. "But God is patient. Heaven has no time limits. It will all come about when God allows it to happen."

That answer was too vague for me, so I countered with, "Why doesn't God just give them the will to change their way of behaving, or why doesn't God just tell them to shape up? All this takes too long for me. After all, we are not on Earth any longer. We're in heaven."

Nancy lifted up her head just shy of looking down on me and said,

"I see you have something in common with these politicians. You still have some problems to work out from Earth. You seem to lack patience. That type of fault will also be done away with as God works on you in due time," she replied.

I didn't like her pointing out one of my faults. I had to struggle with faults long enough on Earth. I didn't have to hear about them in heaven. I guess I had the mistaken idea that in heaven everything would be easy, and qualities like patience, endurance, forbearance and other personality issues to which we aspired on Earth would come automatically in heaven. How little we know.

Feeling a bit miffed, I decided that if I had any other questions, I would get back to Nancy after I talked to some of the local pols.

While walking around, I heard a small group in session debating an issue that appeared to be of great importance to them. What could that be? They had already held elections to determine who was to lead the committees in the political group. So that was not an issue. They had also voted on an agenda, as well as who was to represent them on the counsel that met with God, although the latter issue had not received the final approval from God.

At least one earthly task was unnecessary. They did not have to go around to other groups to do any fund-raising. It was not permitted, and besides, money did not exist here in heaven. On Earth, the accumulation of money is a major preoccupation of any political group. It is the lifeblood of any campaign. When laws are passed prohibiting the so-called hard money being raised by any organization, political luminaries figure out ways to get around the law. By means of one surreptitious maneuver or another in the form of unreported, so-called soft money, the groups manage to build up enormous funds.

Well, the fun of figuring out how to fool the government and get around the law does not exist here. These groups had to be reminded that there were no checks, stocks, bonds, funds, cash reserves, "walking around money" or any other currency in heaven, let alone political payoffs. That was not easy for some of the political types to understand and adjust to.

I kept asking my question about the issue being debated. It took a while to get an answer, as the folks I asked seemed reluctant to give information. That reminded me of the political types I ran into on Earth, who had the habit of not answering questions directly. They commonly "talked around corners."

But here I finally hoped to obtain a direct answer. Here was the question being debated. Should the various political groups go to other groups in heaven on a daily basis and have meetings to get support for their particular issues? The biggest concern was the need to have delegations meet with other groups and with God directly in order to make their political wishes known. The fact that in heaven no crises existed and all needs were already met seemed to elude them. They had been so geared to the process of demanding the satisfaction of some lobbyist's wishes that they could not refrain from continually acting as though the situation in heaven was just like the earthly pursuits they remembered.

I walked up to a tall good-looking man who wore a three-button suit and had a shock of silver gray hair. He had chiseled features that any politician on Earth would have envied – right out of central casting. He looked like he might know what was going on in heaven. I introduced myself to him, and he said his name was Brad. I pictured him as a senator on Earth. He seemed cordial and willing to talk.

"Brad," I said, "Can you answer a few questions for me about what goes on here in heaven?" I didn't tell him about my role as ambassador for God, because I was sure he would begin to flatter me and work on me to put in a good word for him with God. I wanted to get the straight facts about this group without being used by Brad to gain political ends.

"What would you like to know?" asked Brad. "There's a lot to do here. I'm frankly surprised by all the work. I thought life here would be a picnic; you know, eat a lot, have a few beers and sit around listening to music. But I found out quickly from others in this group that there are a lot of issues."

I made the comment, "My understanding is that there are no problems in heaven of a political nature. God has things under control and there is no need to organize political events and issues. Nancy told me that I was on to the truth about the group, but that people here have ingrained in them a way of life, practiced on Earth, that propels them to create issues and go on the offensive to try to solve problems."

Brad looked at me with suspicion. "I don't know what you are talking about. You remind me of some of my constituents on Earth who never believed me when I told them that there was a severe economic or tax problem. They seemed blind to the issues; I and others had to waste our time e-mailing them and sending them literature about what was happening in the country. It's the same here. Folks in the other groups do not think that there are any political problems in heaven. So, it is our job to inform them of all the things that need changing.

"You seem to think that everything here is perfect, and that nothing needs to change. You may not know this, but there are a lot of unhappy people here in heaven. Take the ISMS group, for instance. They have strong beliefs and want everyone to have the convictions they have, whatever they may be. So our group could help them in petitioning God to deal with them fairly."

I couldn't let this go. "Are you saying that God isn't fair with this bigoted group and that you are going to help God with these problems?"

"Well, we think we should be arbitrators between those folks with strong beliefs and God, who wants to change them to become loving congenial people, who freely accept and allow everyone his or her own beliefs," said Brad.

I countered with, "I do not think God needs any help with this. It is up to the people in the ISMS group to find their own way, to soften their criticism and admit that they don't have a monopoly on truth. Besides, I was told that the prophets and saints go there regularly to try to moderate their narrow view of heaven."

Well, I could see that we were not going to get any meeting of the minds on this subject.

I concluded that Brad was stuck in Earth-mode and needed a lot of education from on high. Heaven's counselors had plenty of work to change the habits and attitudes of the members of these political types. I saw that there was no use staying here any longer, since I was not going to change Brad's mind on what he was challenged to do. I thanked him and went on my way.

I thought of the groups on Earth that were not represented here. There was no need for "right to life" contingents or "choice" advocates, since there was no sex or pregnancy here in heaven. The death penalty was not a part of the conversation in heaven, except for members of the ISMS group. Many of these folks had the conviction that all who did not believe in their particular ideology or religious brand of theology should be condemned to hell.

There were no labor unions or teachers' unions with their associated lobbyists. Antiwar rallies did not exist. Neither were there any Save the Whales groups or global concerns for saving the planet. "Green" supporters were not seen anywhere.

So there was little for the political groups to do. It was evident in their frustration with the situation.

Even though God knew all about how the political groups operated, I still felt it was my job to report to Him what I had learned.

I couldn't wait to get to the lawyers' group, as I imagined they had a lot in common with the political types.

**"It is curious that Jesus did not select
his followers from the political and
religious elite. Rather, He chose the
common fisherman, the tax collector
and the tent-maker."**

Richard Roukema

CHAPTER 10

As I roamed around to see what other groups I could find, I came to what seemed like a mountain. I never conceived of there being mountains up here. But there it was, not Mount Everest, but an imposing peak nevertheless. I wondered what could possibly be the point of a mountain in heaven. Would anyone want to climb mountains here or go skiing?

As I climbed up the trail, I realized that the mere thought of bringing myself to the top was all that was necessary to get me there. When I reached the summit, I saw the most exclusive club in heaven. It consisted of Jesus' immediate followers, THE DISCIPLES' CLUB (DC). Even here there was a postscript in large letters: MEMBERS ONLY.

The exclusivity of this group reminded me of the time I went to California in the mid-1960s with my wife and young children. While riding along the coast on the bluffs overlooking the Pacific Ocean, we unexpectedly came upon the site of Esalen, the avant-garde group that was on the forefront of the movement dedicated toward individuation, self-discovery and seeking the center of a meaningful life through meditation.

I expected the group to welcome strangers with open arms. Instead, as we approached Esalen, we were met with signs like "Keep Off, Private Property, NO Trespassing, Violators Will Be Prosecuted." Not a very welcoming message. The warning struck me as inconsistent with the basic intent of the movement.

Here in heaven I was initially turned off by the "Members Only" sign, but I soon realized that only the immediate followers of Jesus were in that group. So I quickly pushed aside my disappointment and was glad to be able to visit with them, as I did have a pass for entrance obtained directly from St. Peter himself.

I knew I would see at least the eleven disciples who were followers of Jesus. It would be fascinating to talk to them. But I noticed that there were far more inhabitants there than I expected to see. So the immediate followers of Jesus were not the first group of men recruited from their fishing boats. Even some of the women who were close to Jesus were there. I thought I would like to talk to Mary, the mother of Jesus, and to Mary Magdalene.

But first, although it made me hesitate a bit, I could not wait to ask if the most infamous disciple, Judas, was among them. Of course, by all earthly accounts of his deception of Jesus, he did not deserve to be there. But considering the long-heralded mercy of God, I thought it might just be a possibility.

When I could not immediately find Judas, I looked around and saw that St. Peter was in charge. You might expect him to be directing things, since he was told by Jesus, "Thou art called Peter, and upon this rock I will build my church" (Matt. 16:18).

Even though he was the head of the welcoming party for new members arriving in heaven, he was also the big man in charge of everything that the disciples did. That got me wondering what St. Paul thought of the choice of St. Peter as leader of the group.

Although St. Paul was not technically one of Jesus' original twelve disciples, he was the author of much of the New Testament and did spread the Word around the then-known world even more than Peter did. At least St. Paul wrote more about it. Maybe St. Peter was more of a talker than a writer.

I also thought that these two disciples were both quite competitive. On the other hand, sins like jealousy and anger may be less prevalent in heaven, or perhaps they don't exist at all. So I guess competition's not a problem. Maybe I'll find out as I continue to visit here.

The disciples were sitting around a table, apparently celebrating the Eucharist, and to my surprise, they were drinking wine. In heaven? How could that be? Again, I think the transition from Earth to heaven is so great that most souls need some of the good Earth's pleasures to get them into heaven's ways of doing things. So wine was permitted, but not abused.

I have long believed that God is not a tyrant. He allows for human error and frailty. He forgives and forgets – well, He forgives anyway. I guess He really doesn't forget.

As it turns out, from my brief stay here, He seems much more forgiving and tolerant than I remember from Old Testament readings. For example, in the biblical story about Noah, I always wondered why Noah was the only righteous man God could find on Earth. So his family was saved from the flood, and the rest of the then-known world had to drown. As a child, I had a hard time with this story. How could God have done that? You may remember, when I talked with God earlier, He said that he had some regrets about some of the things he had done to the people on Earth. Well, maybe even God can mellow with age, or at least change.

In the group celebrating the Eucharist were others not

specifically mentioned in the New Testament as disciples. These included Timothy, Titus, Philemon and Jude. As there seemed to be still more present at the meeting, I surmised that membership in this elite group was not as strict as I had first imagined.

I had to ask Peter about whether Judas was ever present at the meetings with the other disciples. Or was Judas condemned to hell forever? For some reason, when I was a child, I wondered why God allowed Judas to betray his Master. When I approached St. Peter with this question, he seemed a bit annoyed. He looked at me somewhat disdainfully and said,

"Why does everyone want to know about Judas, as if he were the most important person here? Don't you remember that he betrayed Jesus with a kiss and turned Jesus over to the Pharisees for thirty pieces of silver? His guilt about his sin was great, and he became so distraught about it, he hanged himself. How could you be so concerned about a sinner like that? You should be thinking more about the rest of us who were so loyal to Jesus and told the world about Him."

For the moment I wondered why St. Peter was so annoyed about Judas.

"Yes, I remember the New Testament story about Judas," I said. "He has become infamous for his betrayal. But isn't God merciful? I thought about the possibility that God would forgive Judas, because without the betrayal, Jesus would not have been brought before Pilate. He may never have died for our sins."

That idea really disturbed St. Peter. His brow wore a heavy frown and his lips were contorted,

"Are you saying that God should forgive a man like Judas, who betrayed His Master the way he did? Don't you believe that God is just and makes it clear what is acceptable and what is not? Are you the kind of person who thinks God has no standards? What do you want, a God who is wishy-washy?"

Calling God wishy-washy seemed like a low point in St.

Peter's vocabulary. Couldn't he have thought of something more descriptive? But his testy retort got me thinking about his own life. I suddenly recalled St. Peter's famous denial of Jesus. Even though Jesus predicted that Peter would deny him three times, Peter staunchly replied that Jesus was wrong. Yet, before the dawn of the next day had begun, and the first rooster crowed, as Jesus had predicted, Peter denied to others that he knew the Savior. God forgave Peter for that sin. Do I dare bring that up to him? Wouldn't recalling this defect be a slap in his face? That would really anger him.

Well, I considered it long and hard. But in the interest of seeking out the truth here in heaven, I had to ask him about his own act of denial. I realized how brazen it was of me, but I felt, or hoped, that in heaven one is permitted a longer lease on pursuing the truth than on Earth. If the truth cannot be pursued in heaven, then where can it be found?

So I went for the big question: "St. Peter, with all due respect, you were honored by God to be the rock on which God built His church, and God has forgiven your past transgressions. It is well known that you denied a knowledge and friendship of Jesus on three occasions. Just why you did this, I will not speculate about. I am sure you had your reasons. But apparently, God forgave you for that great sin. Judas did not deny Christ. He identified him to his enemies and gave Him up for capture." Of course, God, in His infinite wisdom, knew that this would happen.

At this point I began to feel anxious about my persistent questions. Yes, butterflies in the stomach do happen in heaven.

But I continued. "When I think about it and consider the essence of your sin, your transgression and the sin of Judas do not seem to be that far apart to me, although the outcome of your sin was different. God was gracious to you and showed His mercy. Has He done the same for Judas?"

In the New Testament, Peter, the disciple, is described as

having a temper and being somewhat truculent and hard to get along with. Here in heaven, he had not lost all of his former traits. What I said to him did not initially go over well with him. He shook his head from side to side. I imagined him saying to himself, "I wish this guy would get out of here, maybe even go to hell." But he quickly gathered his emotions and presented me with a view that explained some things.

"You are right about the fact that I denied Jesus. I will have to admit that and can't believe that I did it. I still think of that time, and it haunts me. Furthermore, I am continually amazed that God forgave me for such an outright and obvious sin. God is truly a God of mercy and grace. He forgave me and He forgave Judas as well. So, Judas is one of us. Like me, he has deep regrets about his sin and realizes that his actions were necessary for Jesus to be delivered to Pilate. It is all part of a grand scheme that God has had from the beginning of time. Although these are some of the mysteries that I can reveal to you, I am not free to tell all, as they have been withheld from me as well. Some day we may know what only God knows now."

I had to marvel at the change of attitude that St. Peter had and how he admitted to me his great denial of knowing Jesus.

I then remembered a few lines from Frederick Buechner's book *The Faces of Jesus,* which I read recently. In discussing this very subject, the betrayal of Christ by Judas, he says,

"There can be no doubt in Jesus' mind what the kiss of Judas means, but it is Judas that he is blessing, and Judas that He is prepared to go out and die for now. Judas is only the first in a procession of betrayers two thousand years long. If Jesus were to exclude him from his love and forgiveness, to one degree or another he would have to exclude us all." That statement is very meaningful to me.

How glad I was to have asked the question. I learned that sometimes it pays to be a "Daniel" and be bold. I just wished that I had been more like that on Earth. Life would have been much more satisfying. Reflecting on the conversation with St. Peter, all I could think of was, God is gracious and His mercy endures forever.

Having left Earth, where they were spreading the gospel throughout the then-known world, the disciples were now in heaven. Like so many others, they no longer had the same mission as on Earth. Some of them were bored, although for only a few moments at a time. Mostly, they were a contented group, as their work on Earth was done. They had only to enjoy heaven and occasionally go to other groups and preach uplifting sermons to those who seemed a little shaky as to their role in heaven. They worked with those who had spiritual deficits and coached them on how they could change to become more Christ-like and more pleasing to God. There was little of their situation that I had to report to God.

*****

Going on to another area, and leaving the disciples, I thought you may be wondering about various nationalities in heaven. As I looked around I saw no Asian, Caucasian, South American, African or Middle Eastern gatherings. No groups of red, yellow, black or white citizens, as in the children's song about Jesus' love for the children of the world. It's not like the United Nations. Not that these various populations are not present in heaven, but they are assigned to groups I mentioned above, so you see them mixed up in various other categories, not by countries of origin or ethnic groups.

The skin color of heaven's inhabitants was the same for all and was like no earthly being. I am at a loss for words to adequately describe it. There was something refreshing about that. It made it impossible to make critical remarks about others because of skin color. That was a huge change from the attention given to skin color on Earth. It seemed like it would help to avoid one kind of prejudice.

After this interesting time with the disciples' group, I moved on to check out the other inhabitants in heaven.

**"Whosoever shall exalt himself shall be abased;
And he that shall humble himself shall be exalted."**

Matthew 23:12

CHAPTER 11

Although there are a number of divisions in heaven, they do not exceed the hundreds. When first arriving here, you have to find your way around until you can comfortably fit into a group, as it was a heavenly requirement that everyone attend and be a member of at least one such group. So I continued to observe.

Another gathering that interested me was the HUMILITY CLUB INC. (HCI). I found them on the top of a hill, where they displayed large signs. The signs read HUMILITY IS OUR FINEST QUALITY, PROUD TO BE HERE. In spite of their prominent location, where everyone could view them, they were a quiet and well-behaved group. They all had large metal emblems on their clothes, which read HUMILITY FIRST (when they were in bodily forms and not just existing as ethereal or spiritual beings).

I was initially attracted to this group because, on Earth, I always had the idea that humility suited me best, and that it probably was one of my finest qualities. But when I reflected on that, it sounded too much like bragging, and in the Dutch community of my youth, there was no worse social sin than "putting on the dog," pretending to be better or more than you were, thus revealing a void in your humility quotient. So I guess this is a group to which I could belong. When I was really honest with myself, I realized that I needed to work on my humility. What better place to do it than here in heaven's HUMILITY CLUB.

It was also clear to me that the HCI needed some work on its own basic concept of how humble they were. Pride appeared to be the very sin that they had been blinded to, and that's a big one. How do you convince a group of proud folks that the trait most prominent in their thoughts and statements is the one they most needed to change? We certainly will require some consulting from the prophets and saints about this enigma.

I think it's remarkable that in heaven there are so many problems to solve. I had the naïve idea that in the great beyond, humans would have all their conflicts and illusions resolved as soon as they arrived there. Instead, I found that most of the folks here had earthly moral hangovers to work out, in order to be acceptable to the Creator. Why could God not just make it easy on all of us and just make us perfect? Then we could rest eternally in His presence. Well, as the saying goes, "God only knows."

Upon reflection I remember having a problem with the concept of humility. It went something like this. When you are young you are encouraged to do well in school, behave yourself and possibly do well in sports or other activities and, of course, compete. In order to do this, one had to have a degree of self-esteem.

The latter often seemed to border on the well-known sin of pride, about which, in my background, we were often cautioned. So, how does one walk the fine line of having sufficient ego to do well and meet your goals, while not succumbing to the sin of pride?

When I was a teenager, successful in winning speed skating races or getting A's in my high school classes, was I allowed to feel proud of these accomplishments or would this border on the sin of pride?

My friend Rich, about whom I wrote in the second chapter, once made a perceptive remark when we were in our late teens. He observed that the people who go around acting as though they are very humble may really be secretly proud of themselves. I remember that even if he were not specifically referring to me, the observation was nevertheless true and may well have applied to me. (Aren't kids at this age supposed to be having the time of their lives and not worrying about whether they are humble enough?) Well, it's a blessing and a curse to be so reflective at such a young age.

There is an old psychological axiom that says that the qualities or behaviors of others that consciously bother us most are often those very qualities which we have repressed in ourselves and are fighting to keep hidden from our awareness. By condemning others, we keep these behaviors or traits from being manifested in our own lives.

If the boisterous, bragging stories told by a person bother me inordinately, it is quite likely that I would like to do a bit of bragging myself. But I repress it in my attempt to be humble. Instead I wait, sometimes in vain, for the compliment about my brilliance or performance – thus revealing a secret pride.

It is certainly possible to be proud of your attempts at humility. Wow! God really made us complicated, didn't He? But that's what makes life interesting.

I talked with some of the folks in the HUMILITY CLUB. After telling one man, named Joe, about my conflicts regarding pride and humility, he said,

"Welcome to the club. I had the same difficulty bothering me when I first arrived here. While on Earth, I had the problem of bragging too much and then feeling depressed when I realized that what I was telling others wasn't true. But after discussion with the group here, I was able to understand it better. I can't summarize it in a few words, but a clearer view of the problem dawns on you as you continue in this learning environment."

Sally, a friendly woman, told me about her problems with humility while on Earth. She said, "I had a terrible time as a teenager trying to define who I was. I vacillated between being a quiet introvert and a flaming exhibitionist. One day I dressed like a frightened high school student; another day I dressed like a call girl. My friends thought I was strange. They did not know what to make of me. For that matter, I didn't either. As I grew older these tendencies lessened, but I was always conflicted between being proud of displaying my physical attributes and appearing modest. Here in heaven, I am learning more about the issue of pride and humility and what is acceptable to God."

That satisfied me for the moment. I thanked Joe and Sally for their comments on the subject. I decided that I had enough problems in this area to warrant a chair in the club. I needed to hear what the old-timers had to say about these issues and how they resolved them. So I signed up and got a schedule of their meetings.

"Physician, heal thyself."
Luke 4:23

CHAPTER 12

My visits to the various groups in heaven were more interesting than anything I had experienced on Earth. With each group there was a new twist, a hidden corner that I had not anticipated. I expect that the same will apply to the other groups that I will encounter in my role as ambassador. If nothing else exciting occurs, I will have had my fill of new and revealing information from those on the other side.

I was still looking for the lawyers' group when I heard a noise from across a valley. It sounded like a group of men and women talking. It was not a raucous sound but rather a controlled hum, like hearing a crowd talking at some distance.

My curiosity pulled me in that direction, and as I approached, I saw signs that gave me notice of the group's nature. Large colored signs – TOP DOCS' CLUB (HIGH IQ'S ONLY) were visible on four sides.

In my early life on Earth as a physician, doctors were ethically prohibited from advertising their skills. But more recently, doctors had blatant ads in newspapers, magazines and on cable TV. They bold-facedly hawked their credentials and medical abilities. As a longtime observer of the medical field, I regularly saw the same pictures of doctors from our local hospital in my daily newspaper. The plastic surgeons led the group. I thought this was a crass way to address the public, and these ads were everywhere. I could not help but reflect on our culture, which stresses outward beauty and attractiveness and promises a youthful appearance through surgery.

While all this self-promotion was happening, doctors bemoaned the fact that their role was no longer regarded by the public as a noble profession. I wonder why? They were more like salespersons in the business world – like the fabled used car salesman. Their professionalism had deteriorated, and many seemed to be advertising simply as a means to increase their bank account. I wondered what the physician of the 1930s would have thought of this advertising blitz.

When I was growing up, the physicians in my area all occupied two-story homes. They had their offices on the first floor and lived on the second floor with their families. I knew no doctors who were wealthy. Only later did doctors move into office buildings to accommodate their specialty practices. Much of this was necessary because of the need for laboratories, radiology facilities and other equipment. But before this expansion of services, I remember one doctor making a house call and giving his patients bags of groceries because the wage earner of the household was unemployed during the Great Depression. Change had to occur, but medical care became more impersonal.

I approached one of the group members so he could give me his version of this time in heaven.

His name was Dr. Ward Johnson. He looked very distinguished. My guess is that he was a surgeon on planet Earth.

"Tell me, doctor, how do you like it here in heaven?"

Johnson replied, "I am totally bored. There's nothing to do here. All my hard work in medical school and residency training is completely ignored here. That makes me feel totally useless.'"

I was curious as to his take on the medical profession on

Earth and the fact that docs were all advertising furiously. I asked Dr. Johnson about this.

"Well, what would you do if you were practicing now? Wouldn't you do the same thing to survive? It's just the way the game is played now."

I then asked, "How do you think the doctors were able to practice successfully before all this advertising?"

"Damned if I know. I can't imagine how a doctor could make a living that way without telling everybody what he does and how wonderful his services are."

I could see that this doc could not look back and understand how it was possible to practice medicine with a code of ethics that excluded advertising.

On another matter, even on Earth, I observed that doctors were often elitist in their attitude toward anyone who dared to contradict them in health matters. Having had twelve to sixteen years of education after high school – in specialties that were completely beyond the average person – many doctors couldn't help but get the idea that they knew more about everything than anyone else.

There were physicians who were not that grandiose, but it seemed to me that it was an occupational hazard – this business of becoming omniscient by virtue of years of education. I remember one of my internist friends, a realist about his own skills, making the comment, "I have never met a physician who thought that he was not a good doctor." Thinking about that comment, I would not want a doctor treating me who did not think that he was good at his work. But in reality, as in any field of endeavor, there are some physicians who are a poor reflection on the practice of medicine. Of course, this never applied to me personally. Yeah, right!

I remember the time, long before the use of alternative health foods and drugs and holistic medicine, when many doctors refused to admit that taking vitamins was of any proven value. The attitude was if you eat good food and watch your diet you are able to get all the vitamins you need. One of my friends later succumbed to his patients' wishes and told them to take vitamins, thinking to himself, why try to prove it to my patients that it's useless. Let them take the vitamins. They're harmless. This physician, as well as many others, finally admitted that taking vitamins, as well as alternative methods of treatment such as acupuncture or meditation, may have some value. Things change. While some of the elitism has vanished, the role of the physician has now become a so-called medical care "provider," thanks to the health maintenance organizations (HMO's).

As I approached this isolated group, I tried to imagine what bothered them most. At first, I had a problem finding someone to talk to about the doctors' concerns. No one seemed to be in charge. It was difficult to identify a leader. Everybody seemed to be an expert. There had been an attempt to form an organization, THE HEAVEN'S MEDICAL ASSOCIATION (HMA), comparable to the American Medical Association. But one of the docs pointed out that if there were no diseases in heaven, what would be the reason of having an HMA?

Others felt it was necessary to organize just in case some lawyers got into the group illegitimately and caused some legal problem for them. This attitude originated from the universal animosity of doctors toward lawyers because of the rapid rise in malpractice suits on Earth. In a recent trend, some doctors had abandoned the practice of medicine to go to law school. This tended to put a dent in the doctor/lawyer controversy.

I walked down a path and came upon an isolated road; there I found Hippocrates, Galen, Pasteur, Harvey, Salk and many other famous physicians sitting around discussing issues that had nothing to do with the field of medicine. They had lived fulfilled lives and felt no need to relive their lives or continue to look for folks in heaven who might have illnesses.

Those residents with an extended tenure in heaven had long ago resolved conflicts about their role and were content to watch and listen to the chatter of the recently-arrived docs. They reflected on their lives and had a longitudinal view of how medicine had progressed over the years. They were content that in their lives they had made a significant contribution to the health of society with the medical tools that were available to them at the time they lived.

But other physicians, who had not been famous or had not had unusual careers, were left pondering what they were going to do with themselves, since heaven was free of disease.

The physicians who were famous for their pioneering work in the past were ignored by others as being irrelevant – meaning old-fashioned. The old-timers were regarded as quaint relics of times gone by, much like antiques, and not as heroes on whose shoulders the future of medicine had been built. The other difference: antiques increase in value with time, while these titans of medicine were considered obsolete.

Most of the physicians in heaven viewed the new and modern doctors as the epitome of success and deserving of admiration. It was in this climate that the physicians were discussing their place in heaven.

There was one significant problem for the newly admitted docs in heaven. The residents there did not stay in their bodies all the time. Quite often, a person could switch from bodily form to spirit just by willing it. That could be very disconcerting to those doctors from Earth who never believed that spirits or even souls existed. Here in heaven, just when you got your hands around a body that was complaining of symptoms, that body would morph into a spirit. And few doctors I knew on Earth had any idea how to deal with the spiritual life. So these guys were a bit at sea and appeared confused.

After much inquiry, I located one physician, named Jack, who had been in heaven only a short time. He liked to dress in scrubs and a long white coat. He looked like the doctor in a laboratory of an academic institution, or the teaching researcher of earthly renown. Jack elaborated on the plight of docs in heaven.

"Doctors have one huge problem. There are no illnesses or diseases, no medical emergencies, no accidents, no infectious illnesses, no cancers, no needed operations and no psychiatric problems among inhabitants here. The doctors have no work to do. So the problem is, what are they to do with their extensive knowledge of the world of medicine? Nothing! They keep wondering how to find a new reason for their time in heaven."

After spending a lifetime helping patients cope with their illnesses, it is a terrible blow to be unemployed. Some even inquired if it was possible to return to Earth to continue their work, where they were appreciated.

Many of the doctors have other interests, and they are spared the anxiety of being without work. But others are completely lost, feel bored and have little energy. Some keep looking around and asking if there are any patients in the other groups in heaven. When told that there are no diseases in heaven at all, they are stunned and in a state of disbelief.

The problem was obvious. What could interest these folks who had spent so much time becoming experts at skills that were no longer needed? The situation reminded me of some doctors on planet Earth who, upon retirement, felt useless and irrelevant. I knew of a few who became clinically depressed and required psychiatric treatment. I knew other physicians who found it impossible to retire, knowing well that they would be very distressed without their work. They continued as working physicians until illness or death stopped their obsession with their medical expertise.

Back here in heaven, I heard one doctor, named Bill, who

was dressed so casually that he looked like he was on his way to doing something other than being a doctor, like going to a ball game. I asked him his opinion of this heaven devoid of patients with illnesses.

He was quick to say, "Just wait. There may not be any illnesses here now, but there will be infections. Looking around here, I don't see anyone paying great attention to cleanliness, such as washing hands. Something is bound to happen. And you know about cancer. It can be obscure and hidden for a while, but sooner or later it shows up. And, being so close to the sun – you know about radiation exposure. We are all bound to have skin cancer sooner or later."

Mike, an atypical doctor here in heaven, overheard Bill's comment. He seemed to have evolved to a level beyond the others and did not need the lost role of the physician. Mike approached us with a smile on his face and a slightly superior manner. He looked at Bill and said,

"Bill, you don't know what you're talking about. You're living in the past. You have to give up your old life. If you understood a bit about theology, which you ignored entirely on Earth, you would know that in heaven there are no diseases. We have to find another reason for living besides being physicians. We just have to do something very different from what we did on Earth." That comment only left Bill befuddled.

One doctor, a drug researcher on Earth, was desperate. He was dressed in a white laboratory coat and looked professorial with his goatee and long hair. His name was Jeff, and he told me,

"There has got to be some need here for drugs. All cancer can't be absent. Endocrine diseases and infections are bound to show up, as Bill suggested. Of course, the confusion here is that everybody looks so healthy, and they are often in a spirit form. I never heard of a spirit getting sick. Maybe if someone is beginning to feel ill, all he has to do is wish to be in spirit form and bingo, he feels fine. It's all very distressing. I wish that on Earth I had discovered some new interests rather than concentrating entirely on my research. It makes me feel like I did when I was in my teens – having no idea what I wanted to do with my life. Now I'm here, and I'm just as puzzled as to what I should do, as I was then."

The discussion went around among many doctors, but none could find a role that suited most of them in the group. It was obvious that the doctors' job in heaven was to swallow their pride about extensive knowledge of the narrow field of medicine and find a new reason for existence in heaven. From what I could gather this was going to take a long time – hopefully not as long as an eternity.

But not all the physicians in heaven were distressed by what they found there. It was now the year 2020, and it had not been the best time to practice medicine. The whole area of diagnostics and therapeutics in the field of medicine had been in chaos for some years. With the Democratic party taking over the control of the House of Representatives, Senate and the Presidency in 2008, the groundwork was set for a national health insurance system, an area to which the government had only given lip service before, except, of course, for Medicare.

The business world was also tired of paying an increasingly higher portion of the medical bill. Historically, when big business and government are on the same page, there is little that will stop such a coalition from having their will. After many plans were submitted for approval, the House and Senate passed a universal health care bill for all citizens. It happened in 2012. This resulted in better care for many patients and some long lines for folks awaiting elective surgery. Also, the issue of rationing care evolved. Everyone who needed expensive surgery such as a heart transplant or even extensive diagnostic procedures could not receive such care. There was simply too much demand for services. In addition, with the cost of medical care free or low, there was a tendency to overuse the system.

An attempt was also made by insurance companies to continue and expand a third tier of medical care for those wealthy enough to afford it. This relieved some of the financial stress on the universal health care system.

Meanwhile, a trend had developed among doctors, with many leaving the practice of medicine and going into other fields. This movement, which started before the turn of the century, had accelerated. Doctors were now leaving the practice of medicine in droves because they were not being paid enough to keep their offices open and because of the high cost and fear of malpractice suits.

Medical schools, numbering well over a hundred at the turn of the century, had dwindled to ninety. Few students competed to go to medical school, since it cost as much as several hundred thousand dollars to graduate from college and medical school. Those who did become physicians were either from lower socio-economic levels and thereby received scholarships or were highly dedicated persons who had only one goal in mind – becoming a physician for humanitarian reasons. Financial compensation was of little concern to this latter group.

But another trend developed and was long overdue. Physicians in practice began to work mainly in supervisory roles or did only highly complex technical procedures. The actual day-to-day medical care was administered by physicians' assistants, nurse practitioners and technicians. Those in academic circles had long concluded that doctors were not needed to treat sore throats and colds and other common problems. The same thing was happening in dentistry. Routine cavity treatments and tooth cleaning were now done by technicians rather than dentists. These changes were a welcome and practical solution to the shortage of doctors and dentists.

An example of this change began during my time in the medical field. When I interned in a general hospital, I was required to ride the ambulance for emergencies, which included accidents, fires, heart attack victims and an occasional home childbirth. Later, all these duties were handled very well by Emergency Medical Technicians (EMT's). It had become clear that physicians were no longer needed as the first line of treatment in emergency situations. Well-trained technicians could do as well as physicians. So much of the medical care that was formerly done by the local family physician or internist was being done by others.

The other problem affecting doctors, mentioned above, was the malpractice issue. Trial lawyers engaged in malpractice suits had become the reigning princes of the legal profession. But the fallout had been the increasing fear of these lawsuits that loomed over physicians, forcing them to practice defensive medicine and pay enormous insurance costs. This condition reached extreme proportions, leading some physicians to leave the practice of medicine entirely.

At one point this caused a temporary halt in medical care for the general public. Across the country, physicians went on strike, except for emergency rooms. After only two days, this crisis motivated the federal government to meet in an emergency session to call a temporary halt to malpractice suits. After months of battling law suits from the American Bar Association, the government passed a bill that made the contingency fee illegal. From then on, anyone who wanted to sue a doctor for malpractice had to pay up front for legal services. This made the law consistent with other advanced countries, where contingency fees do not exist.

Malpractice suit rates fell to about 5 percent of their previous level. When lawsuits went on too long, arbitration panels were consulted to adjudicate the case.

Following this unusual punch to the jaw of the legal profession, all bets were off and gross changes were made to the practice of law. Even in other areas of legal actions, lawsuits were markedly diminished for fear that the government would react in a similar fashion and further restrict the lawyers' activity. This was a remarkable change in political thinking, since there are far more lawyers in government than any other vocation.

Some of the doctors in heaven were glad to rid themselves of the problems on Earth, and they had no issue with not working as physicians in heaven. But many were restless and were continuously talking about being useful in some way. So, it was clear what they had to do in heaven. The doctors needed a dose of reality and had to orient themselves to a new existence and find a new reason for being.

Among some physicians, there were signs that this was beginning to happen, but it would take a long time to have all of them make the adjustment. Some of the docs had taken an interest in heavenly music. Others began an interest in philosophy or theology – admittedly, very new to them.

While I enjoyed my work as a physician on Earth and had no regrets about entering the field, I found early on that socializing exclusively with physicians was not as interesting as mixing with a variety of people in different fields of work, such as business types, artists, writers and others. Socializing only with doctors seemed to me too limiting both socially and intellectually. So why would I want to join the doctors' group here? I doubt that I would like the preoccupation with their agenda here any more than I liked their exclusiveness on Earth.

Well, I wanted to report back to God. Of course, with all the groups, God was far more aware of the problems than I could possibly tell Him, but I felt it my responsibility to file a report anyway. One thing I was clear on: I did not want to spend my heavenly time among my colleagues and grouse about not being able to work as a doctor. I had long ago resolved that issue while still on Earth.

"To see over the next mountain
To travel beyond the horizon
To wander about strange lands
This is the dream of the adventurer."

Richard Roukema

CHAPTER 13

In a valley, among what looked like an autumn scene of brilliant color, almost hidden in a dense forest, I found the ADVENTURERS' CLUB, (AC). They were a restless group. Many never seemed to tire of exploring the territory. If you wanted directions to anywhere in heaven, they were your go-to-guys to give you info on what's where and how to get there. Unlike others here in heaven, they seemed to have global satellite positioning sensors in their heavenly brains, and they were never disoriented.

While expecting to see famous explorers all around, to my surprise, the first person I saw was Cain, the son of Adam and Eve, the Old Testament bad guy, the murderer. Wow! Cain! How could he be in heaven? After all, he killed Abel, the first recorded murder in biblical history. Does God allow killers in heaven? How inclusive can He get?

On the other hand, although Cain committed what many consider the ultimate sin, when he killed his brother, nowhere during Cain's time, was there a record in the Bible that the taking of life was wrong. How was he to know that it was a sin, and that he might be subject to severe punishment? Had God spoken to this issue yet? Is this why the mark was placed on Cain's forehead, to acknowledge his sin, as a warning to other living creatures on Earth that killing was not approved of by God? A mark on your forehead was hardly a death sentence. I can't figure this one out.

The Bible has certainly left us with many more questions than answers. This is another matter I will have to bring before the saints. I began to wonder where I came up with these ideas. I am certain that others have questioned these subjects before, but I have never read or heard about such matters.

Cain probably traveled far and helped populate parts of the world, which made him eligible for the ADVENTURERS' CLUB. To our knowledge, he did not go around killing others in those biblical times. Maybe he wasn't all bad. Perhaps he learned from his experience, and there was a reason for him to be here in heaven. Who are we to judge?

Among the early explorers were the great Marco Polo, Christopher Columbus, and Henry Hudson, as well as many of the early explorers. I also saw some of the modern explorers – Perry, Byrd, Lindbergh and a few of our astronauts.

I could see how these guys would never tire of talking about their voyages on Earth or in outer space, and how the wanderlust gene stayed with them in heaven. Everyone there seemed to be a leader. So it was difficult finding someone with whom to talk, just anyone who was not fixated on telling his story.

I finally found Marco Polo, who was willing to talk in a general way about this interesting group. After all, he had been in heaven so long, he didn't need to talk about his adventures to every new person he saw. He was dressed in the old explorer's costume, with boots, knee pants, shirt and cape. Nearby he had animal skins just in case the weather changed and it became cold, which never happened in heaven. He had been caught unawares many times in his extensive travels and suffered unbearably cold weather. Marco wasn't taking any chances.

"Marco," I said, "you conducted a most remarkable feat with your travels. I could never imagine making my way to the Orient like you did under such primitive conditions over years of traveling. You were amazing. How ever did you do it? What gave you the determination and strength to go the distance?"

"It wasn't easy," replied Marco. "We had many trials. At times we were near starvation for lack of food. At other times, along various trade routes, we had more than enough to eat and drink. There were also periods of intense heat in the deserts and extreme cold in the mountains. But our goal was to get to the East and find spices, gold and whatever other valuables we could discover. Through it all, it was the sense of adventure that kept us going.

"But let me tell you, I was raised in the Catholic Church in Venice, and I carried my faith in God with me. It got me through many a perilous journey. At one time the great Kublai Khan wanted to hear more about Christianity than he and his family had known before from other Christian travelers. I tried to bring two Dominican priests along on a trip. However, they became sick and dispirited; they couldn't take the journey and had to go back. But my party and I told the Khan all we knew about Christianity. My faith in God was essential in helping me and my traveling parties with the difficult journeys."

"I appreciate what you are saying about how God helped you. I want to hear more about your travels. Perhaps we can get together, when we both have more time to sit back and relax over a glass of wine. But, for the moment, can you tell me how the folks here in the Adventurers' Club are getting along, and what they are trying to do?" I asked.

"Yes, I can," replied Marco. "The explorers here are very

restless and want to continue going around looking for new places and discovering new lands. When I first arrived in heaven, I had the same problem. But after wandering around for years, I found out that every place here is similar to other areas. The landscape changes a bit, but it has nothing like the infinite variety we all know on Earth.

"There is no need to explore heaven. The newcomers take a long while to catch on to this. They keep thinking that things here are the same as on planet Earth. This makes them very distressed and restless. They just can't seem to believe that every area of heaven is much like any other. Their wandering around doesn't do any harm, and it keeps them busy. But there is nothing for them to do. Eventually, they will find their way and relax about it all."

I was satisfied with this explanation, but another explorer, who had sailed with Columbus as part of the crew on the Nina, approached me and said,

"I heard you talking to Marco. He's well adjusted here, but let me tell you, I think God could do something to correct this situation for us. I have been here a long time, and I'm still not used to sitting around all day. Exploring is in my blood, man.

"God can't just have us do nothing. He should know better than to expect us, who have such restless souls, to just sit around and simply be idle. None of us know music, art or anything that the others may be doing. I don't know what God expects of us. I understand that you are an ambassador to God. Could you ask Him about this?"

I replied that I would try, but doubted that I would get any helpful info. from God about this issue.

Although it would be fun listening to them tell their tales, I realized I couldn't fit in with this group. I was not very adventurous in my days on planet Earth. While still there, my only daring trip was hitch-hiking, round-trip, from New Jersey to Arizona in order to attend college at Arizona State College in Tempe. I thought I was being a really bold traveler, but my attempt pales by comparison to the great explorers of history and hardly qualifies me to be one of heaven's adventurers. So I knew I could not join this group and be part of it.

It was clear to me that those in the adventurers' group had a tough job in their mental backpacks. They had to give up their restlessness, do some daily walks to get over their need to move about, and settle in to a more contemplative life. Not an easy task for this group.

There were other groups in heaven. For example, the builders, carpenters and architects who arrived here were as restless and eager to work as any other group. They couldn't wait to get their hands on the "many mansions" that Jesus talked about. They somehow had the idea that they would be busy building McMansions, but one of God's staffers quickly disabused them of these fantasies, as there was no need for these overly large, ostentatious homes in heaven. As a result, these construction types were under great stress as well.

They were constantly going around looking at existing buildings and making suggestions as to how improvements could be made and how a building could increase in value if such work were done. They were convinced that many of the small homes were potential "knock downs" that could be replaced with large homes with many unused rooms. But their recommendations had no takers in heaven. They, too, were unemployed. For this group, as well as others, it was very difficult to get on with heaven's program.

Another large group was continually looking for work – these were the maids, housekeepers and au pairs. I often saw these service people dusting clouds and cleaning the stardust that seemed to settle on the landscape. But, in fact, none of this was necessary. The winds of heaven normally whisked away any stardust or celestial debris.

Furthermore, there were no children to care for. As I said earlier, if a person in heaven wanted to be a child or adolescent, he or she could will it and in an instant re-experience being younger. But the adventure to childhood seldom lasted long. Most of heaven's inhabitants wanted to be adults.

There was little for the housekeepers to do. For them, the change to heaven was not too difficult, since the task of cleaning on Earth was very hard work and giving it up was not that difficult. With time, this large group was learning to relax and adjust to their new role in heaven. They were actually beginning to enjoy it.

There was another group I saw in heaven. They were the business types. You can imagine how frustrated they were. There was nothing to sell, no bargaining on houses or cars, no cash only deals, no stocks, bonds or any other financial instruments to sell.

With a mind set toward building a company or a large personal fortune, these folks were completely at sea in heaven, like farmers without seed or water, like the docs without patients or the lawyers without clients. Most of them had not bothered with the contemplative life on Earth. They were too involved in business to be concerned with "that stuff."

However, some business types did pause in mid-life to wonder why they were so attached to accumulating wealth. They had heard the saying, "You can't take it with you." On Earth they began to live a more leisurely style and find enjoyment in music, reading or various sports. Many began to follow the familiar advice, "Take time to smell the roses." These folks were on their way toward taking a look at their more spiritual side. In heaven, they had a head start on developing some other goals. They needed less counseling help from the saints and prophets.

Again I drew up my report to God, but I doubted that it would be at all informative to Him. Just doing my job.

"Power tends to corrupt and absolute power corrupts absolutely."

Lord Acton to Bishop Mandell Creighton

CHAPTER 14

Perhaps you, too, feel uncomfortable with the most powerful group on Earth, who now found themselves transferred to heaven. This group gives me the creeps. They are in the RULE THE WORLD CHESS CLUB (RTWCC). The earthly rulers – the kings, presidents, imams, rulers of all kinds – were here sending out their knights, pawns, yes, even bishops and others to fight their battles. In heaven's wisdom, they were fortunately relegated to a game of chess instead of the furious wars and battles they directed on Earth.

Few of these old rulers ever put on a uniform to fight an earthly battle themselves, at least not in modern times. Even as a child, I never understood why these powerful political types were always allowed to send out young men and women, at the peak of their lives, to fight wars for these leaders. As you might expect, here in heaven, these potentates sat at the chess tables pushing around board pieces in a continual war for dominance.

On Earth, it always astonished me how the Islamic terrorist leaders were able to convince young people to blow themselves up, ostensibly for rewards of pleasure in heaven.

I always wondered when Islam's youth would challenge their leaders to do the evil job themselves, rather than put it all off on the young. It is amazing to me that young men and women throughout the world are not more revolutionary toward the older folks in their society. The oldsters always want the young to do their dirty work.

At first, I wondered how these guys were permitted entry into heaven. Certainly, they were not among the most virtuous of God's children. Something is going on here that I fail to understand. There are too many bad guys in heaven. Judas, Cain, warriors of all kinds, fearsome leaders who cared little for those killed in battle. Many other unsavory characters were here as well. How was this possible? Maybe this is a sort of purgatory and many of these bad guys are headed for hell eventually, and it just hasn't happened yet.

Isn't there any justice? Is there not a Judgment Day, as mentioned so often in the Bible? Or does God save all those that He created, who lived on Earth? If that's true, then there must be absolutely no limit to His grace. It's all very confusing. I thought that in heaven everything would be clear and all our earthly doubts and questions would be answered immediately.

Life here would be so much more pleasant if we didn't have to think about these questions all the time. I remembered reading the story of Jacob wrestling with God in the Bible. Now I find that we have to do the same thing here instead of relaxing on a cloud free of Earth's existential problems.

So, I thought of looking for Jacob (later named Israel by God), and asking him about this problem. I had to recall the group where he usually hung out. Finally, I found him and approached him about the evil leaders on Earth and how they were able to reach heaven.

Jacob looked much like I imagined he would. He had a white robe which covered his short pants and brief sleeveless shirt.

He had a long beard that was snow white. He did not look like a fighter. Rather, Jacob had a kindly manner, a rugged face, but with soft eyes.

I began to wonder if he was still ready to wrestle anyone with whom he disagreed. Had he overcome the pugilistic attitude that he displayed on Earth? Well, when I engaged him in my questions, he seemed very relaxed and reflective – not at all what I expected.

"Jacob," I said, "you were a rather famous person in the Old Testament. You had a lot of courage to challenge God as you did, and I thought you might be the one to ask about how all these bad guys ended up in heaven."

"Yes, as you may know, it is common in the Old Testament to argue with God about the events on Earth. It has always been a tradition in the Jewish culture to argue and challenge God about the more difficult moral questions. But as for outright evil, God has always been against that. God had to be very clear on what acceptable behavior is, and what is sin.

"Jesus tried to clarify the issue in the hope that the Jews of his day would appreciate the finer points of the law. He wanted the Jews to attend to the spirit of the law and not just the letter of the law. That's why he had a big problem with the Pharisees. But there never was a problem about the Ten Commandments, in which it was clear that killing, stealing etc. was wrong. Neither Moses nor Jesus ever differentiated between one sin and another. All sin was condemned. So it is questionable if God regards one sin as being worse than another.

"I know that as humans we cannot comprehend this, as we certainly would regard killing to be much worse than, say, lying or stealing. God sees it all as sin; it is only through His mercy that any sin is forgiven. So, when you see these rulers of the world with their great armies sending troops off to kill or be killed, they are not sinning any worse than when a leader commits a personal sin.

"To us, it just looks worse because of the numbers. You may remember that in the Old Testament there were many wars that God supported in which the Israelites were favored in battle. Was God sinning when He favored His people? I tried to find out the answer to this while here in heaven, but so far no one has been able to give me a satisfactory reply. There are just some things that we may never understand. God's ways are often inscrutable."

Suddenly, I thought of the most infamous killer of all, at least in my lifetime – Adolph Hitler, the Fuhrer. And then Genghis Kahn also came to mind. Where were they? I had not seen them, nor had anyone talked about them. Were they in another group? I could not think of them qualifying for any other part of heaven's subdivisions.

I had to ask Jacob about this enigma.

"Jacob, what about Hitler and those who were as evil as he was? They can't possibly be in heaven."

Jacob was quick to reply, "You raise a good question. I haven't seen or heard of Hitler. I really don't know where he is. If God's grace goes so far as to excuse him as well some of the other worst sinners, then I too will be surprised. I'll do some asking around for the answer and get back to you."

Well, that was disappointing! If Jacob didn't know, I wondered where he would get the answers. Not knowing where these bad guys were might mean that hell really exists and they are suffering, receiving their just reward forever. But somehow that seemed too simple, and not in line with what I had learned in heaven about the fate of God's creatures.

After making the above comments, Jacob shrugged his shoulders and smiled. At that point it did not seem worth pursuing the issue further.

I don't think I am going to get the answer on this problem

soon. Then I remembered that most of the other groups here had earthly attachments to activities that preoccupied them in the previous life. It got me thinking that in heaven it takes time not only to reach perfection, but also to learn what God has in mind for each of us.

God, having infinite patience, may simply wait for us humans to come around to His expectations. I just wish that God would give me some of His patience, so that I could relax more about these things.

Well, the RULE THE WORLD CHESS CLUB had a long way to go. They were still into fighting battles, even if they were only struggling over chess. Members of the saints' group and the disciples' club visited with the world rulers and tried to convince them that there was more to life in heaven than winning chess games. My guess with this group – considering their massive egos – is it will take a long time for them to appreciate any message conveyed by the prophets and saints of heaven.

"An epiphany is God's gift to the reflective soul."

Richard Roukema

CHAPTER 15

While still on Earth, driving home from Vermont one day, I viewed a scene that most folks have witnessed at one time or another. As never before, this day I had an epiphany.

Looking to the south, I saw an abundance of variegated clouds which had followed a rainy interlude. The sun was shining through the clouds creating beams or shafts of light that spread for miles.

If these were stairways, they would have appeared as walkways through the clouds, as if to heaven.

Thoughts ran through my mind – peaceful and contented thoughts. I reflected on the scene – yes, another way that God manifests Himself through nature – a beautiful scene of clouds and rays of sunshine that went on for many moments.

As I was lost in contemplation, I recalled a high school assignment. It became rooted in my memory by virtue of our teacher asking us to memorize a passage from Tennyson's *La Morte d'Arthur* in the *Idylls of the King*. As King Arthur stood on a barge and prepared to sail away prior to his passing from the Earth, he offered a soliloquy: "The old order changeth yielding place to new, and God fulfils Himself in many ways, lest one good custom should corrupt the world."

It is surprising that here on Earth some institutions created to preserve truth and promote helpful ideas become icons or symbols of that truth and often lose the meaning and significance of their original verity. History reveals that this is true for many political ideologies and governments as well as philosophies and religions.

As an adolescent, I saw this in the various splits and factions in the Protestant church – Lutheran, Baptist, Methodist, Episcopal, Missionary Alliance etc., I could go on.

As an adult, I witnessed similar divisions in the psychoanalytical arena from the orthodox Freudians, Jungians, Adlerians, and Sullivanians, the existential schools and later the various cognitive approaches. Each of these groups saw truth in their individual concepts. Each played a role in our understanding of the human mind, yet none of the various schools of psychoanalysis or psychotherapies had the last word in how the mind functions.

The same tendency is true of other areas in which humans are engaged. Groups have found it necessary to codify and establish a government, a church, or an organization in an attempt to define their beliefs and goals. Eventually, these newly-formed groups become rigid in form and lose the brilliance and imagination of their founders.

This was one of the primary complaints and critiques that Jesus had of the Pharisees, the religious ruling body of His day. They lived the letter of the law, in its many forms and rituals handed down to them over the centuries, but they missed the spirit of the message.

Prehistoric humans worshiped the sun, the stars, Earth, animals and images of various kinds. Rather than worship an ethereal god, they felt the need to deify their object of worship, such as the sun. The Greeks and Romans worshiped many gods and wrote about them in their myths and created images of them in statuary.

The Old Testament is full of worship gone awry. Whether in the case of the tower of Babel, the worship of Baal or the golden calf, God's people had to be constantly reminded that they were missing the mark – worshiping concrete forms or symbols rather than the spiritual nature of God.

In Christianity, God sent His Son in the form of a man to become the Savior of humankind. Although other religions have deified humans in some form, never has a religion claimed that a Son of God became Man in such an overt manner.

So the question – hardly original – is what happens to those who have never heard of Jesus? Are they cast into Hell? What about the Jews, and countless other peoples who existed before Christ? Do they have no salvation because they did not know Him?

The severely orthodox of any religion have one thing in common. They believe that they have found the ultimate truth and that all others have not. Each orthodox faith has its true believers. Those outside of orthodoxy are the unfortunate folks who will not be saved – whether they are nominally Islamic, Jewish, Christian, Mormon, or any other religion that is exclusive in its orthodoxy.

And so it goes. I am reminded of the fable of the blind men and the elephant. Each man felt a different part of the animal and was convinced that the part represented the whole of the elephant. Feeling the elephant's leg, one blind man concluded that the elephant was much like a tree. Another man, feeling the tail, said that the elephant had to be like a rope.

Could it be that each society at some time in history saw a part of God as He/She revealed the God-self to humans and declared, indeed, that what they observed was the essence of God to the exclusion of all other representations of God?

Modern folk, at least in Western cultures, seem to have given up on polytheism. If there is a belief in God, it is generally in monotheism or perhaps in a Force or Prime Mover. When observing the heavens, the planets, stars, galaxies and the deeper universe, it is hard to imagine all of this existing without some controlling factor, be it some primordial force or a personal Deity.

But humankind has a way of wanting to make things simple, to codify, to concretize, to conceive in absolute terms, thus eliminating doubt; hence the tendency toward the outright origin and invention of orthodoxy.

As orthodoxy arises, doubt is repressed and minimized, thus strengthening the faithful to continue to seek those of like mind.

Among the orthodox, as in the Christian and Muslim religions, attendance at group meetings in churches or mosques is usually high. Among the less orthodox, attendance is less rigid, and the need for constant confirmation of "truth" seems less necessary. With this latter group, there is more tolerance of doubt and less need to compulsively conform to the institutional requirements of a religion.

These are some of the ruminations that ran through my mind as I continued to drive down the highway.

All civilizations have formed their particular orthodoxy over the centuries. Could it be that God, in His infinite wisdom, sent the Old Testament prophets throughout the years to remind the Jews and us, living today, of our failures in orthodoxy – of abiding to the letter of the doctrines and missing the original truths of the religion?

Christ certainly was incisive in pointing out the hypocrisy of the Pharisees. Paul elaborated extensively on the spirit of the Christian faith – that salvation comes by faith and not by works. This later became the central point of difference that Martin Luther had with the Catholic Church, whose hierarchy had stressed good works as a testament to one's faith.

Dare I say that the Muslim faith came to address areas of living that Christians were ignoring? Even the present orthodox Muslims practice a strict form of religion that is not unlike what Christian Fundamentalists do (no alcohol, rules about dress and sexual behavior).

Of course, the extreme terrorists of the jihad movements of recent years have belied the truths found in the Koran, or so it seems to me.

When feudalism was rampant throughout Europe in the Middle Ages, the Catholic Church reigned supreme in Europe. Did God send Luther to point out the sins of the Church, the hypocrisy, the misuse of funds and the repressive nature of the church? Did this movement, in turn, sharpen the faithful toward a more Christ-like behavior?

And now for a giant leap! Did Joseph Smith, the founder of Mormonism, remind us of how we were failing as Christians, and in some manner show us a better way?

The Mormons, like all of us, fail to be exemplary in thought and deed in a variety of ways, but as a group they appear to lead a more moral life than the general American public. Of course, many non-Mormons would object to the lack of equality for women in the Mormon Church, as compared to men. And because they believe that their founder was privy to tablets, uncovered in upstate New York, that form an additional "word of God," they are condemned by many in orthodox Christian circles as heretics or cultists.

Many observers have said glibly that there are certain truths that are part of all religions. Who could deny that this is true? But does that mean that each faith is in itself equally worthy of our attention and belief?

It appears that the particular faith that a person chooses is usually consistent with what he/she has been taught from childhood. Of course, there are exceptions. A good example is St. Paul, who was converted from Judaism to Christianity on the road to Damascus. I personally know folks who were reared Christian and later became committed to Judaism, and vice versa. Although there are many instances of conversions to various faiths, most humans have adopted the faith of their fathers and are not troubled by invitations to believe in other doctrines.

Could it be that God reveals Himself in many ways religiously to each culture, since we are so different that no one form of religion would appeal to us all? Does God give us the opportunity to discover truth where we fit in best? Certainly this thought is heresy to any orthodox, believing, religious person of any religion. And again, it is hardly an original flow of ideas.

But by what hubris, conceit, selfishness, and disregard of others do some humans conclude that they have the ultimate truth – an exclusive, inside relationship with God, and that all others are worshiping false gods and false beliefs? Many leaders of the major religions of the world have proclaimed that he or she has the final word from God and that others are false. So what is one to do?

Am I saying that all of this is a matter of relativity – that picking one religion or another does not matter? Not at all. As for me, there is no other possibility that I could chose anything but Christianity. But neither does it mean that I must demonize or look down on all others who do not believe in the Christian faith.

Our minds are too narrow to conceive of the big picture. We do not know what will happen to those of other faiths.

We who accept Christianity by faith do not know for certain what will transpire when life no longer exists for us in earthly form. We live in the hope of a heaven. But what of others who subscribe to entirely different religions?

To paraphrase Tennyson's King Arthur as he leaves on the barge, perhaps **God reveals Himself in many ways lest one good *religion* should corrupt the Earth.** Is that too heretical a position to take?

*****

As I saw the streams of light coming down to Earth from the sky, while still driving down the highway, I thought of the various ways in which God manifests Him/Herself to us humans.

It gave me comfort and a feeling of peace and well-being that perhaps He reveals something of the God-self through various religions as well as in many ways in nature. Even the evil that exists in man is not possible without God permitting it to happen.

Should we view everyone – the good, the evil, the not so good – all as parts of what God had in mind to help us search for some truth? To make us marvel at the mystery that is the diversity of behaviors seen in humans?

All the above came to me as an epiphany, a sudden insight into the nature of faith and existence. Much of it has, no doubt, been said before in so many ways, but when it bursts into one's personal awareness one day, it seems to provide a ballast for the future, an awareness that helps to soften the hard edges of daily life.

When I arrived home that day, there was a copy of *Books and Culture* in the mail. This magazine is published by *Christianity Today.* As I paged through it, I came across a review of seven books all on the above theme. The article is called "Jesus and the Religions." It discussed at length the concept of pluralism, exclusivity and inclusivity.

One of the books is quoted as having "an open inclusivism that holds to a deposit of faith in Jesus Christ that contains implicitly everything of religious significance but recognizes that the Church may learn what some of these implications are from those outside its boundaries such as scientists, economists, and practitioners of other religions." (Paul Griffiths in *Problems in Religious Diversity.*)

I find myself leaning toward inclusivism and away from the orthodoxy of exclusivism.

To put it simply, as humans we are privy to so little of what God and the universe is all about. The chances are great that we are observing, feeling, touching and conceiving of only one part of the universal elephant.

Only our insecurity and, to some extent, our narcissism lead us to resort to narrow doctrines. God and the universe seem too complex. Existential issues are not that easily dismissed.

After this long dissertation of various religions, I hope you haven't forgotten that we were "walking all over God's heaven." Let's go call on the ALL SAINTS RETREAT.

**"Though idolized when in heaven, most saints
Were far from perfect on Earth."**

Richard Roukema

CHAPTER 16

Back to my dream. As I looked over a plain to a pleasant hilltop, I saw a town, shrouded in white. It reminded me of traveling in Italy some years ago. While driving through the countryside with my wife and another couple, we came upon the town of Assisi.

Viewing it from a distance, it looked like a mirage. Upon nearing the town, the white buildings came into view. I was pleasantly surprised that here in heaven the retreat for the saints looked much like how I remember the town of Assisi.

There it was – the ALL SAINTS RETREAT (ASR). It was a relatively small area with several individual buildings, numerous birds filling the air and every variety of flowering plants. Risking the comparison, it really looked like another heaven.

As you might expect, St. Francis of Assisi was in charge, but St. Peter was also there, along with some other disciples.

You will remember that the disciples had their own club. But it was clear that one could join several clubs without any problem. The wonderful thing was that you could be in three clubs at one time and attend all of them simultaneously and not miss a beat. It was truly wonderful to be a spirit, if you preferred that to being in a renewed body. And the length of time in spirit or body had little significance here.

Since there were relatively few members at the retreat, I rather quickly ran into St. Augustine, St. Thomas Aquinas, St. Francis of Assisi and a number of the Popes.

Needless to say, I felt quite uncomfortable here; belonging to this elite society was out of the question. They were far too intellectual, theological, philosophical and much too devout for me to qualify. But I was curious as to what they were talking about in their conferences.

The whole setting reminded me of an earthly retreat. The accommodations were spartan, and each guest had to follow the traditions that had been in place for centuries. There were long tables with benches for those who were in physical form. The food served was very basic with few flourishes. I could identify boiled chicken and rice, a few raw vegetables; unlike in other groups, the guest had no choice of menu. It reminded me of a monastery I visited in Macedonia a few years before.

The aura of the ASR was that of simplicity. No frills. The surrounding countryside with its great variety of birds and flowers held sufficient beauty on which to contemplate the nature and wonder of God.

I walked up to St. Thomas Aquinas and noticed that he still looked as described by biographers: a big man with a large head, referred to affectionately as "The Bull." He had a kindly face. I looked directly at him and asked,

"Sir, I noticed that you seem very much at home here. I want to ask you about the agenda at the ASR."

"Son," he said, "let me tell you about some of the past that preoccupies the folks in the ASR. For example, the Popes and the other religious leaders who were alive during the wars of their time, often ask here, in heaven, whether these conflicts were necessary. They are particularly upset about the Crusades, although many of the Popes authorized and supported these wars. At the time, it all seemed like a holy war, done for the glory of God. But looking back on it, thousands of citizens were killed. There was rape, pillage, theft and all manner of crime done in the name of religious faith."

When I heard St. Thomas Aquinas talk about the religious wars this way, I could not help but think of what is happening in the twenty-first century. Doesn't what St. Thomas described sound much like the holy Islamist jihad that is going on now throughout the world? They are trying to justify conflict in the name of Allah, while some of the leaders in our country also want to portray the conflict as a religious struggle – as good versus evil.

So I asked St. Thomas Aquinas, "Is there such a thing as a holy war? Even the wars of the Old Testament are hard to justify, even though we read in the Bible that God was often on the side of the Israelites. Was the Old Testament time really different from our modern age? Have old customs and traditions been so far removed from today's life? Can all values and morals of the Old Testament times be translated directly to the modern era? Has civilization not made any progress? Are we not more civil in our worldwide discourses and decisions?"

Feeling a bit challenged by my questions, St. Thomas Aquinas said,

"Although I cannot answer all of your questions, it is interesting to speculate on this matter. All the laws of the Old Testament are not applicable today.

"For example, restrictions on food, attitudes toward women, and the permissive attitudes toward polygamy and slavery, to mention only a few, are all traditions that are not still honored in many cultures."

I then asked, "Since Old Testament times, has God changed

His mind on the acts of war? Are there justified wars? Should we have fought the first and second world wars or the revolutionary war? Is all war evil? Is all killing evil? Should we outlaw the death penalty? Is it time to reevaluate what is moral and what is not?"

St. Thomas Aquinas took a deep breath in response to this onslaught of questions. He replied,

"God does not wish humans to kill each other. One of the commandments specifically forbids it. But atrocities, such as the massive killing of Jews during the Holocaust, had to be stopped. Such gross killing of one group by another cannot be tolerated. It became necessary to kill some individuals from the offending countries in order to right this situation. Obviously, there are exceptions to the law against killing, and this was the most notable.

"Of course, I cannot answer these weighty questions alone. These are some of the issues that the ASR is discussing."

I decided that although I had nothing in my background that would qualify me to be in this elite club, I would, nevertheless, ask permission to attend retreats simply to listen to the saints discuss the challenges that morality presented in light of what has transpired over the ages. I cannot think of anything more interesting to listen to than discussion of some of the greatest moral issues that the planet has encountered.

I asked St. Thomas Aquinas about this.

"Let me tell you," he said, "we do allow exceptions to those who are interested in these subjects, both in an intellectual way and spiritually. But we want assurance that guests would not request a presence here merely out of curiosity, like some paparazzi. We do not want someone reporting on what transpired in the ASR as a form of gossip to other groups, who might be tempted to be derisive of our efforts to deal with these difficult issues."

I thanked St. Thomas Aquinas for his cordiality to me and went on my way. I walked out of there slowly, keeping in mind the stimulation of being among saints who were dealing with weighty matters. I looked forward to revisiting them on another day.

"Attorneys, like physicians, are not revered until there is need for them."

Richard Roukema

CHAPTER 17

This time I was determined to get to the lawyers' club. I should have known how to identify them. They are among the loudest here in heaven, although the arguing in the political group compares favorably in volume.

The lawyers' group occupied one of the most exclusive locations in heaven. It was not just given to them by a generous God. They negotiated for it over time. Initially, they were relegated to a distant part of heaven, away from the center of activity. The attorneys wanted a more prominent location. In some sense, exact placement was not essential – unlike earthly locations, since God was always available in His spiritual Self, occupying all areas of heaven at the same time. That may be hard to imagine with a planet Earth mindset, but it's the best way I can describe it at the present time.

After many negotiations with St. Peter, God's representative in the "deal," the lawyers settled on a beautiful spot on a hill with lush vegetation and copious wildlife. This setting may not seem very suitable to lawyers accustomed to lavish offices with extensive libraries, computers and meeting rooms, but it was satisfactory to the lawyers. Besides, the beauty of the surroundings was conducive to reflection and possible spiritual growth.

I suspect that St. Peter and God placed them in this rural setting in order to bring them close to basic life forms, namely animals and fields full of flowers and other beautiful plants, thus hoping to turn them away from their mental, verbal and visceral habits and toward a more contemplative life. When I first came upon them, it was obvious that the location had no appreciable effect on them as of yet. But God is patient.

As I approached the area, I couldn't help but notice the large signs. One marked the location of the HEAVENLY BAR ASSOCIATION (HBA). Like the doctors' HEAVEN'S MEDICAL ASSOCIATION here in heaven, they had to form an organization similar to the earthly American Bar Association. There were other signs – HEAVEN'S MOOT COURT as well as the CELESTIAL LAW REVIEW. Both these organizations served to help the lawyers adjust to heaven's new conditions.

In HEAVEN'S MOOT COURT, newly arrived lawyers could relive law school successes and eventually have a means to segue to other activities. It mainly kept them busy, so that they had few initial complaints upon arriving in heaven.

The lawyers who were more academic and creative joined the law review. This had a real purpose – namely, to clarify what heaven requires for the regulation of life, the pursuit of happiness and a minimum of justice for all. This required a degree of arrogance on the lawyers' part, as though they could really negotiate with God about their role in heaven's ways.

If I checked with the saints, I am certain they would tell me that the attorneys are still in Earth mode, thinking they can bring a suit in court to affect the outcome of anything conceived of as injustice. They will eventually realize that they don't have much to say about the rules of heaven. It's all up to God. But as with other groups here, it will take a long time to give up a lifetime of work habits and attitudes formed on Earth.

As I looked around, I wanted to inquire about whether any notable lawyers were there. Alice, one of the women, who appeared to be serving as a hostess for visitors, looked like she might have some answers. She was well dressed in a business suit and appeared ready to take on any legal challenge that heaven had to offer. The problem was that litigation did not exist. Alice had a determined face, a confident walk and a pleasant smile. I approached her with my questions.

"Alice, looking around here, I don't see any really well known lawyers from planet Earth. They certainly must be here."

"Yes, many of the famous attorneys of the past are here. You may not always recognize them, as some have gone to wearing togas rather than business suits. For example, you might recognize those two men over there sitting on the wall talking. The one on the right is Clarence Darrow, the other is William Jennings Bryan and behind them is Abe Lincoln." There were many others from the distant past, but Alice did not know their names.

I asked, "Would you introduce me to one of these famous attorneys?" She said that she did not know them well, but would attempt to get an audience with one of them.

Alice approached President Lincoln and to my surprise, he readily agreed to speak with me. He looked the same as the pictures of him on Earth. He was tall and gangly, had a black beard and was dressed in a formal suit. He had a kindly manner. I approached him with enormous excitement. Having been awed by the great statue of Lincoln in Washington, D.C., I was struck by the likeness of the president himself to the statue, as if he had just moved from that great marble chair and come to greet me.

"Hello, President Lincoln, I am so pleased to meet you. I have often visited the Lincoln Memorial, and always admired what you did for our country. You have been such an inspiration to many."

"Thank you, sir, but it was only with God's help that I was able to cope with the tremendous problems which existed when I was on Earth. It takes a lot of help from others as well to effect change in cultures that have strong or misguided values."

"Tell me, do you find yourself thinking like a lawyer here or are you more inclined to think of yourself as President?" I thought that this was the pivotal question to ask of the great man.

The president looked gracious and very benevolent as he spoke.

"When on Earth, I was blessed with many challenges and God gave me many successes. He also helped me through the frequent depressions I suffered resulting from the difficulties of my job; He pulled me up from despair when family tragedies occurred. When my life was cut short by an assassin's bullet, I had already lived a full life. My work on Earth was essentially over.

"Here in heaven, I have no need to continue being a president or an attorney. I am in this group by choice so that I can help the other attorneys see a way of being in heaven that is not all about arguing cases and winning lawsuits. This refers especially to the newly-arrived lawyers. They are so Earthbound; they habitually want to get into controversial issues. They have to understand that there is a spiritual dimension to life here in heaven that is more about love of others and being thankful to God for His blessings."

Although I wanted to engage the President with more conversation, I did not want to take up more of his time. I thanked him for his wise comments. It made me reflect on those persons I know who have lived a fulfilled life and contributed much to society in their work. These folks retired from their labors and then lived a contemplative life full of satisfying reflections, while continuing to give to others of their energy and talents. After living such complete lives these individuals are ready for heaven.

I went on to talk to others. I thought it would be best to talk to some of the lawyers that had recently arrived. Soon I located a rather young woman who had come to heaven prematurely. I was told her name was Brenda. She had been a trial lawyer, who had died in an auto accident only months before. She looked attractive in her business suit with her briefcase held closely at her side, as though she was about to enter a court house and defend a client.

"Brenda," I asked, "how are things for you here in heaven? Are you enjoying yourself? Do you find interesting things to do?"

"Are you kidding? This place in a real disappointment! There's nothing substantial to do. I'm used to busy days, arguing in court and winning cases. Here, all I can do is pretend I'm doing something important by going to moot court. That's for young kids who are still in law school. I have had twenty years of intense experience in high-powered courts. There's nothing here that compares to that. It's a real drag."

I was a bit surprised at her comments but it was easy to catch her disappointment. I had to ask,

"Haven't you found the pace here easier and more pleasant?"

"Who needs 'easier,' and what's so wonderful about 'pleasant?' What I need is action – an adrenaline rush. What gets my juices going is a case I can get my teeth into, one that gets my blood boiling. Here there is nothing like that. I wish there were something I could do to get revved up. Even a drug might help. There are some older guys here who are trying to get me to settle down and do other things. But so far, they have not come up with anything that appeals to me."

"I guess it takes time to get used to heaven's ways. I hope

you will feel better as time goes on," I offered.

"I have plenty of time. But who needs time, if there is zilch to do," she replied.

Brenda was really stuck in her Earth mode. I saw that this conversation was going nowhere, so I moved on. I approached a man who looked like he might be willing to talk about his experience here.

I introduced myself to the man, named John, who was dressed in a jacket and tie and khaki pants with a bevy of pens in his shirt pocket. He had the rotund look of a well-fed, middle-aged man who was more inclined to sit at a desk than run marathons. John told me he had been a real estate attorney. I asked him how he found the conditions in heaven and how he spent his time.

"I find life here somewhat boring. I'm used to working hard, arranging things for people to be home owners. I looked around to see if there were any plots or houses for sale, but I was told that God never allowed any sales activity. I would like to keep busy, but singing praises to God is hard, as I was always a monotone and couldn't sing to save my life.

"I've been advised to try to contemplate the nature of heaven, but honestly, I don't know how to contemplate. Nobody taught me to do this in school. I wouldn't know how to begin. Maybe one of the old-timers will clue me in on how to go about it. Somebody said that meditation was good for you. But I don't know beans about meditation."

I could understand John's dilemma. If you were not by nature contemplative, it might be a hard activity to suddenly learn. It made me think of the many folks who never meditate or reflect on what they do in their lives. They are more action-oriented and seldom look back on what they have done or what its significance might be. How different we humans are. In heaven, some of these same earthly traits, which are not useful in heaven, seem to persist and need considerable adjustment when one crosses over to the other side.

I decided to visit moot court to see how the young lawyers were doing. What a show! I thought I was viewing Court TV. The group had to fabricate cases about issues, such as contract law or malpractice, as there were no genuine legal problems here. But even though these were legal problems that had no reality in heaven, the lawyers on either side were aggressive and posed their arguments with vigor. The fact that they were in heaven had not made a full impact on them as of yet. Yes, they knew they had arrived and had left Earth, but their spirits had not absorbed the significance of their new life.

The saints made frequent visits to the lawyers' group. They had to make the meetings with the attorneys compulsory, as given the freedom of choice to attend the sage advice of the saints, the lawyers seldom showed up.

I talked to a prominent attorney named Brian, who had a commanding presence about him. He was tall, slim and had a sharp, chiseled face. I guessed that he had been a trial lawyer on planet Earth. I asked him about meeting with the saints.

"Look, man, I don't need anyone to tell me to meet with anyone. Do you realize that on Earth I participated in famous legal cases? The newspapers were filled with compliments on my legal skills. And I made big bucks doing it. Then I come here, and the first thing I am told is that I have to meet with the saints to get advice – to get with the program. Who needs advice? Not me. I always relied on myself to do things. I never needed advice from anyone. What I need is a few good cases to get my teeth into. That's what makes me come alive."

Well, one thing was obvious in talking with Brad. He certainly didn't have a problem with a sagging ego. Dying and passing to the other side didn't put a dent in his self-esteem.

I had to ask him, "Brad, when you were on Earth, I am certain you frequently consulted your library, and in recent years, you used the Internet to learn from cases that resembled what you were working on. There were precedents of law to which you referred. You didn't invent the legal decisions each time all by yourself. You had to rely on the legal minds of the past to use in your current cases. Can you see that the saints, having been here a long time and being experts in spiritual matters, might know something that you had not thought of, and that they may be helpful in heaven? After all, this is a new place and a new experience for you. You are not an expert on heaven.

"I talked to the doctors a while ago. They seemed to have a similar problem in that they thought their vast studies in science and experience with disease made them experts on everything. As a result, they were not at all eager to adapt to heaven's ways. Forgive me for being so presumptive as to make this observation of your situation in heaven. Maybe a few conversations with the saints would help you make an adjustment here."

I took a deep breath after those comments, as I was afraid I had insulted the legal mind that I was confronting. But to my surprise Brad said,

"Well, I don't expect much to come from talking with those old-timers. They don't have a clue as to what's going on in the modern world. But I guess it wouldn't hurt either. I don't have anything else to do."

I thanked Brad for his time and went on my way. I talked to other attorneys who had a broader view of things. A number of them, while on Earth, had straddled the avenue dividing secularism and religious concerns. They seemed to have a greater appreciation of possible assistance they could receive from the prophets and saints and were more open to suggestions.

Now as you know, lawyers have a way of finding loopholes in any argument.

They are trained that way, and with time, they become especially skilled at it. So why would you expect them to suddenly change in heaven? It takes time to alter traditional earthly ways of thinking and behaving. I have hopes that they will change, but it is such an ingrained trait. I wonder what tricks God has up His ethereal sleeves to undo "lawyer think."

It was apparent that some of the attorneys had a lot of work to do to meet God's requirements for perfection in heaven. Like all the other groups, except for the saints, the prophets and the disciples' group, they needed time to alter their old habits obtained from years of indoctrination of earthly tradition in their particular field of endeavor. I suspected that the other groups I hadn't visited yet would show similar patterns of immaturity in God's eyes. I wrote up my report on the attorneys' group and filed it away on heaven's virtual Internet.

"Persons in the gay community frequently refer to others as homophobic. Does that make the gay community heterophobic? Or would it be best not to call each other names?"

Richard Roukema

CHAPTER 18

If you have my curiosity, you may have wondered why I had not mentioned the group which on Earth causes so much fascination and is, to many, the most troublesome area of life. I am referring to sexual orientation. Here in heaven it is called the all-inclusive SEXUAL PREFERENCES AND INDENTITY CLUB (SPAIC). All the arguing and bickering of earthlings are here resolved eventually – sooner or later.

When I first encountered this group I was quite surprised. First of all, it was hard to find. One of the angels gave me directions. I had to go quite a distance, which of course is no problem here, since I had only to wish that I was there. But the SPAIC was off the beaten track, as if they did not want to be bothered by visitors. This may have been a residual tendency left over from planet Earth, which often regarded some members of this group as peculiar, strange, or in some cases unwanted persons. Eventually I located the club in a beautiful valley with remarkable vegetation and comfortable homes.

For a while I walked around and contemplated the struggles these folks had on Earth. I did wonder how they arrived in heaven, given all the religious proclamations and condemnations on Earth against anything but "normal" sexual behavior, meaning, of course, heterosexual orientation.

You may recall the biblical story of the cities of Sodom and Gomorrah, which were destroyed by fire because of the sin of their inhabitants. It is presumed that the destruction was because of the homosexuality that was practiced there by at least some citizens. In Genesis 19, we read about a crowd of men who came to Lot's home to ask him to release his houseguests – two angels – so that they could engage in homosexual acts with them. Lot, in his attempt to persuade these men to leave the door of his house, even offers them his two virgin daughters as a substitute for his guests, so that the intruders might have sex with them. Parenthetically, can you imagine that such an offer would be made in our present day?

Later, the two angels tell Lot that God has sent them to destroy the city, and that Lot and his family should leave as soon as possible, before the city is burned down. Lot hesitates, but the angels take him, his wife and daughters and they leave the city. The city is then burned to cinders, and the term "sodomy" is born, signifying a sexual act that is regarded by many as abnormal and sinful. Lot's wife turns around, looks back, perhaps thinking about her losses, and she is punished by being turned into a pillar of salt.

Throughout the Bible, as recorded in Leviticus and especially in the New Testament, there are references to the "unnatural acts" that men performed with other men. As a result of these biblical condemnations, many Christians regard homosexuality as sinful behavior and totally unacceptable to the Christian life.

In recent years, some folks who are homosexual, whether male or female, have spoken of their practice as a "lifestyle choice." I think that this was an unfortunate use of words meant to normalize homosexual conduct. Such a phrase sounds like a preference made by them, not unlike preferring living in the city rather than residing in a rural area.

This idea of choice seemed to energize the Christian conservatives to further condemn the practice, because it was viewed as a deliberate act of will.

I can recall folks on Earth in the conservative Christian community saying:

"Those who live as homosexuals could choose to be heterosexual if they wanted to. They simply practice 'unnatural acts' because of a deliberate choice, and therefore are disobedient to God's will. I have heard of cases where homosexuals converted to heterosexuality through prayer and faith. They could change if they really wanted to. They just prefer to keep living in sin."

Some less conservative Christians and a large section of the secular population on Earth have a different view of these sexual behaviors. I have heard these folks say something like this:

"A certain percentage of the population, ranging from 3 to 8 percent, according to studies done by scientists, have been attracted to the same sex from their earliest memories. Furthermore, these same individuals have no sexual desires at all toward the opposite sex. Therefore, their sexual thoughts, fantasies and behaviors are not a matter of choice, but are rather the result of an innate biological drive that cannot be altered. The exact reason for the difference in sexual preference from the rest of the population is not yet known.

"Some scientific studies have suggested that hormonal changes occurring before birth may have an effect on sexual preference. Studies done on animals suggest some validity to this."

An unknown number of the human race is apparently bisexual – able to have sexual intercourse with either sex. The reason for this tendency is a puzzle to investigators and may be partly biological and partly psychological.

Members of the gay community who have affiliations with religious institutions have maintained that they can be practicing Christians, Jews or members of any other faith and still be engaged in a gay relationship. They stress the love that can exist between two men or two women who are committed to each other in an ongoing relationship.

It has been noted that Jesus never made any statements about homosexual practices in the recorded gospels. The implication of this is if Jesus felt it was of great importance, he certainly would have mentioned it, as he talked about many sinful behaviors but never mentioned homosexuality. On planet Earth the controversy continues among religious groups.

The question here in heaven was whether God resolved this issue in His eternal wisdom. Or had it not as of yet been resolved? As noted in the other groups in heaven, whatever a group's problems were on Earth, the issues are not all completely solved in heaven, necessitating a good deal more heavenly work toward the goal of perfection, aided by counseling from the prophets and saints.

I looked around at the members of the SPAIC group. There seemed to be no leadership. I enquired about this, and it was confirmed that there was a lack of direction, and that they depended heavily on their counselors for assistance. I understood that, but I wasn't certain that the prophets and saints would have an historical view of the problem, since the morality of Old Testament and New Testament times was quite different from what is going on today.

I will note only three examples. The first is from biblical times, when there was rampant polygamy practiced by the wealthy, which was not condemned by the Old Testament prophets.

The second example is the acceptance of slavery in both Old and New Testament times. Nowhere is this condemned as an immoral act against other human beings.

The third example is from Genesis 19. After Lot leaves Sodom, his wife is struck dead because she looked back at the city burning. Lot then moves to a small town with his two daughters. (As a child, and even now, I never understood why death was necessary for merely looking back on the city). Lot's two offspring want to have children, and for some reason, they cannot find suitable mates. So they both seduce Lot with too much wine, have sex with him and each conceives a child so as to have an inheritance. That's an amazing way to have children.

If such an act were discovered today, it would certainly be regarded as a criminal act with major consequences. But the Bible does not make any comment about the daughters' behavior. It merely explains that as a result of their incestuous conception, the children of Lot's daughters founded the Moabite and the Ammonite nations. Clearly, the moral standards acceptable centuries ago are not in accordance with the moral values today.

I ruminated long over the most appropriate person or persons to ask about the sexual preference and the homosexual issues noted above.

I decided to go with an earthly technique that always managed to spread out responsibility. I appointed a committee. Well, at least I would ask a group of the notables in heaven to work on these problems. I figured I would get one of the old-timers from centuries ago, one of the early Christian saints, another from the medieval times and one or two who were acquainted with modern thoughts on the subject. This group ought to resolve any issue that might evolve from discussions. To my surprise the following folks accepted my challenge.

King Solomon, the son of David, noted for his great wisdom, power and wealth seemed like a good choice. Solomon is said to have built the first temple in Jerusalem. The Bible tells us that he had seven hundred wives, princesses and concubines – enough to keep him very busy. In his dotage, his wives persuaded him to seek out other gods, which displeased the God of Israel – Yahweh (1 Kings 11:4).

In his wisdom, he arbitrated between two women, each of whom claimed that a young child was her offspring. He offers to cut the child in half with a sword. The mother of the child resists this and is willing to give the child to the other woman, rather than have the child killed. Solomon decides that since she was not willing to have the infant killed, she must be the actual mother. He gives her the baby.

Solomon is credited with authoring the book of Ecclesiastes, the Song of Solomon and the book of Proverbs – books which represent some of the finest of biblical literature.

It was not hard to enlist Solomon for my project, as he wasn't too busy. He readily accepted. I had to be careful in our discussions not to get on the subject of polygamy, as he was probably the prime example of that practice in his day. I had to avoid slavery too, of course, since he had an abundance of slaves.

Solomon looked like a seer and a man of wisdom. He had a close-cut beard, flowing hair, a robe and sandals, although he had none of the accoutrements of royal acclaim such as a crown, gold rings and lavish clothes.

I needed others for opinions on the issues at hand. Next, I contacted St. Paul, who I found wandering around still embarked on some kind of missionary work, which in heaven I thought was unnecessary. He had on a robe and sandals, and around his neck were the remnants of a few strands of leather that he used for his tent making. He looked quite tense – not the person I had imagined, one who had run the race and fought the good fight. He looked tired, and in earthly terms, in need of a good night's sleep.

When he heard about the subject to be discussed, he looked at me and asked,

"So what's the problem? I spoke to that a long time ago. I doubt that anything has happened to change my mind. But I'll come anyway. Maybe it will help the others, when they hear what I have to say." To St. Paul, there was no big problem, no issue. His lack of humility was striking.

St. Paul had recognized the problems that sexual drives were causing among his newly-converted Christians. He railed against promiscuity, fornication and homosexuality. He advised men to marry if they could not control their sexual urges, but hastened to add that to really serve Jesus Christ, it was better to remain a bachelor.

This reaction to sexual urges appeared to herald or at least influence the later practice of celibacy practiced by Catholic clergy. The monks/priests were said to be the representatives of the Church, and the latter was symbolically the bride of Christ. St. Paul regarded sexual drives as more of a troublesome nuisance to the spiritual life than a life force to be honored and used in appropriate ways.

With St. Paul's limited view and experience with sexual problems, he was hardly the ideal person to consult on these matters. However, in light of his well-known missionary work and contribution to the New Testament in the form of his letters to his churches, I felt he should be included.

After a brief search I located St. Augustine and asked him to join the group. He had been a less-than-exemplary Christian in his younger days. He was born in North Africa (present-day Algeria) and although he was raised Catholic by his religious mother, he choose to engage in sexual experimentation for some years before his conversion to Christianity. He had a son by a woman with whom he lived for some fifteen years. He obtained an extensive education in literature and studied rhetoric.

He later studied and taught in Milan, where his mother persuaded him to marry. However, he had to wait two years until the woman he planned to marry came of age. Meanwhile, he was sexually involved with another woman, during which time he uttered this prayer: "Grant me chastity and continence, but not yet." Shortly thereafter, he read about St. Anthony of the Desert, after which he underwent a conversion to Catholicism. He then gave up his teaching and study of rhetoric and entered the priesthood.

The details of St Augustine's life are chronicled in his autobiography, *The Confessions.* In his book *The City of God,* he took an extensive leap into theology and a speculative view of activities in heaven. His extensive writings (*On Christian Doctrine)* and other commentaries and letters greatly influenced Catholic Church doctrine and the Reformers, Martin Luther and John Calvin.

St. Augustine was known for his tendency to be reflective. I thought he would be a good person to attend my group. He readily agreed to come.

Then I thought of St. Thomas Aquinas, who was a great moralist and scholar. He might have a centered view of things, and given the problem I will pose to him, he might have some interesting views. Like St. Augustine, he had written extensively on theological issues in his *Summa Theologica.* When I asked St. Thomas Aquinas to join the committee to talk about sexual orientation, he had a scholarly reaction to the issue and readily agreed to come to the meeting.

My biggest problem was choosing a modern day saint. I think that when you are living with personalities of your time it is difficult to determine who is saintly. We usually know too much about individuals who have lived recently to list them among the saints in heaven. I was in a quandary.

After much thought, I decided that whomever I chose, be it a recently deceased Pope or a noted theologian, they would have fixed views of the subject and probably would not have much to contribute that I did not already know. I decided to forgo the contribution of a modern day saint and go with a composite of modern earthly views. Although not an expert in this field, I am familiar with many of these views.

I couldn't wait to get together with the famous men of old. Then it suddenly occurred to me that I had not thought of including a woman. Besides being politically correct on this subject, I thought that women might have a somewhat different view of the issues of sexual orientation. I venture to say that women may see a more human, emotional flavor. But who to ask? How about Mother Teresa? She had died recently and was being considered for sainthood by the Catholic Church. She would quite likely bring the old saints down to basics, much like Jesus Himself had done.

I found Mother Teresa extremely busy here in heaven. She had not been able to slow the pace that she set for herself while on Earth. She was still wandering around looking for the poor, the sick and the downtrodden – none of whom were to be found in heaven. As a new arrival, she had not yet learned to enjoy the true nature and meaning of heaven, and was still functioning in Earth mode. But she was very interested in the subject at hand and readily agreed to join the group.

Since I had chosen a modern woman to participate on the committee, I had second thoughts about not including a modern theologian. After talking to one of my colleagues, I decided on Karl Barth. He had been a famous Protestant Swiss theologian, well known enough to Americans to have his picture featured on the cover of *Time* magazine some years ago.

Barth was also a relatively late arrival in heaven and appeared very busy. Having been a professor for years, he was trying to get on the lecture circuit but was having little success, as there was no market for lectures in heaven. In addition, like some of the others, he had written extensively about the Christian faith. He was more familiar with the sexual preference issue than the others and was more than willing to join the group.

How's that for a committee? Wouldn't you like to have a tape recording of the conversations coming out of that group? Lacking a verbatim report, I will do the best I can to summarize their comments.

After much negotiating for a day that we could all get together, I finally was able to arrange a meeting of the six notable committee members in a place where we would have some privacy. I did not want an audience; no hisses, boos or applauding. I wanted this to be a considered, deliberate, intellectual discussion, free of the rampant prejudice and politicizing arguments so often seen on planet Earth. Maybe that was too much to ask, but I figured that without striving for high standards, I may never get anywhere with this sensitive subject.

To begin the meeting, I deferred to King Solomon. Although he did not live the most ideal life, according to God's law on Earth, he was known for his wisdom. The books of Proverbs and Ecclesiastes attest to his sage-like status. So I asked King Solomon to begin the discussions. He agreed and called the meeting to order.

"Gentlemen and lady, we are gathered here to discuss the issues of sexual preferences and homosexuality. I will begin by saying that things certainly are very different on Earth now than when I was there. Since the days of the early Hebrew writings and from the stories of Lot and the destruction of Sodom and Gomorrah, it was clear to most of us that sexual encounters, male to male, were not approved by Hebrew law.

"I don't remember much being said about women engaging in intimate behaviors. So, as for myself, I would like to hear what the others have to say. I am open to changing my thoughts on the matter if it can be shown that new discoveries have been made in this difficult area."

The idea of an Old Testament sage being open to the possibility of changing his mind about Hebrew law really blew my mind. But this was Solomon. He had thought through many of life's existential issues. He was not one to come to judgments quickly. I suspected that as he aged and considered the puzzling aspects of life, he became less certain that he had all the answers. How refreshing; even Solomon did not have complete wisdom on all issues.

St. Paul was quick to enter the discussion. He referred to his own writing in the New Testament, in which he severely condemned homosexual acts.

"When I was on Earth, there was much sin, especially in the sexual area. I tried to get the early Christians to live an exemplary life, based on faith in God and respect for the commandments. I knew God's law about adultery as a sin, and if that was forbidden, certainly sexual acts between two men were sinful. So, I spoke about it often, because it was going on even among the early Christians. I never had the slightest doubt that God did not want mankind to behave this way."

Forgive me for a diversion from the committee discussion to a comment about St. Paul. Like many others, I have wondered what St. Paul's problem was when he comments in his writings about his "thorn in the flesh." Was it a physical affliction like arthritis or epilepsy or was it a sexual problem? Was his celibacy easy or did he have to struggle with it on a daily basis? Was he sexually attracted to women or possibly directed toward men? Of course, we will never know. Some writers have said that St. Paul was "obsessed" with sexual sins, while paying no attention to other commandments and social inequities such as slavery, which was generally accepted in his time by those financially able to afford slaves.

Sometimes I think that I have too many "aside" thoughts. It certainly doesn't make things easy for me. It makes life difficult, even here in heaven. But I guess I am condemned to be this way – or is it blessed?

As I expected to have many provocative comments from St. Thomas Aquinas and St. Augustine on the subject of sexual inclinations, I was surprised at their lack of depth on the subject.

St. Thomas said that the sexual sins had never preoccupied him very much, as he was not in constant turmoil over sexual impulses.

"I must admit that I had very few problems with sex, as it never was my most difficult area. I had more trouble with pride and had to struggle daily with it. When I wrote extensively on theology, I wondered whether I had the monopoly on religious thoughts. I had to ask myself if I was not just a bit grandiose to write so extensively all those volumes on theology, as if I knew it all. Was I writing another Bible?

"The other sin that bothered me a great deal was anger. It always seemed to me that anger was much more prevalent than sexual sins, although I must admit that I didn't pay that much attention to sexual sins. Sexual intimacies between men did not occur to me as a major sin, although I could not see it as a normal thing to do. I remember wondering how God could create humans who would be attracted to the same sex. As I said, I never spent much time thinking about this as an issue. There always seemed to be so much more to occupy my mind."

At this point Karl Barth broke into the conversation. He actually lived through a time when the "gay movement" became a political reality. He had seen it as part of the liberalization of sex in the early 50s, as it became more and more accepted by society and even among some Christian and Jewish groups.

Barth began, "I lived in a much different time than most of

you did, and the issue of sexual behavior has become much more complex. At first glance, sex between members of the same sex, be it men or women, seems to defy the original purpose of the sexual life. The most conservative among religious thinkers believe that sex is only for propagation of the race. Very few are in that camp. Most respect the notion that the sexual life also includes the emotional factors so important to a successful relationship between two people and is not merely for propagation of the race.

"On the other hand, most religions condemn promiscuity and support monogamy. But as time has gone on, considerable debate has occurred on the subject of monogamy as it relates to homosexuality. A small number of Christian clergy have endorsed homosexual behavior and have declared homosexual unions as appropriate and compatible with the Christian life.

"These clergypersons argue that the enduring, loving relationship between two individuals is the important ingredient, not the sex of the two people. While promiscuous sex would not be acceptable in religious communities, long-term intimate and loving behavior may be seen as consistent with Christianity. The other thing that is new is the research that is being done on the issue. It has become quite clear that a significant number of persons have never had any sexual inclinations or attractions to the opposite sex. Why? Well, the exact answer to that is still not known. There may be genetic, psychological and environmental influences responsible for inclinations toward the same sex. More research is needed to help clarify these issues."

All this was news to the previous speakers, as they had lived in earlier times. As I looked around the group, I could see a mixture of doubt, consternation, wonder and deep thought among the committee members.

St. Augustine wanted to talk and King Solomon readily gave him the floor. The early Christian saint, recalling his early debauchery and his later confessions, was quick to say,

"I had considerable problems with my sexual urges. I had no homosexual inclinations and did not really understand the attraction to men. However, I was not that far removed in time from the Greeks and Romans, who engaged in homosexual practices, where it was not uncommon for adult males to have sex with young boys. Homosexuality was not frowned upon in that society the way it is today. As I said, I could not really understand such behaviors, having no drive in that direction. Also, I could not see any way to rationalize it as a Christian practice. I saw it as an act of will that could be countered by deciding not to engage in sex with men. Why couldn't men simply have sex with women?"

I have always admired St. Augustine, but on this subject he seemed remarkably naïve. I'm sure it had something to do with the time in which he lived, but his lack of depth on the issue was disappointing.

When King Solomon deferred to Mother Teresa as the last speaker, I suspected he did this unconsciously. There is no way that he could have overcome his innate feelings that the feminine gender was inferior and deserving of less attention. His patriarchal background precluded him from being fair to the only female member of the committee. I guess the unconscious operates in heaven much like it does on planet Earth. As a psychiatrist, I found that very interesting.

But Mother Teresa was very gracious. Having played second fiddle to many a man on Earth, she had long ago relegated this phenomenon to male chauvinism.

She had put it in the category of things that for some men will never change. She only hoped that the other committee members would be a bit more gracious about it.

She took a deep breath, pushed down her brief feelings of annoyance, and followed the discussion with these comments.

"As with my colleague Dr. Barth, I too have lived in times when the matter of sexual preference has been the topic of much discussion. Personally, I have never had much trouble with the sexual urge. It has not been a constant struggle with me, as I know it is with many persons. Besides, I saw my work as so urgent and necessary as to put aside all thoughts of personal gratification of the body. I saw so much hunger and poverty that it seemed to me these conditions were much more important than whether one person was attracted to another sexually.

"I saw so much disease, including the relatively new one – AIDS – so prevalent in countries such as India and Africa. I was aware of how this disease is contracted, but I had little sympathy with those who thought God was punishing sinners for sexual acts by giving them a fatal illness. How dare they speak for God in such matters! I saw many little children caught in the stream of illness due to their parents' acts. Are they to be condemned too? Where is the mercy that Jesus asked of us? Why are humans always in such a rush to judge the actions of others?

"I don't know the answer to the homosexual issue, but I am listening to what folks are saying about the love between two people as being more important than the sexual act. While on Earth, I knew practicing Christians who had long term, committed relationships with members of the same sex, and I respected them. However, I have not yet seen a satisfactory solution to the whole problem."

It was interesting to hear what Mother Teresa and the others had to say. I then remembered that I had not asked them about the issues of sexual identity. This is a subject that has become prominent in recent years. I am sure that others were aware of it in the past, but it was not a subject that the public was alert to until recently.

While still on Earth, I recall talking to a young girl of twelve whom I had been asked to see in my psychiatric office. She stated categorically that she had always felt like a boy, and that she was determined to be a boy. She had started to develop the female physical attributes of a girl and did everything she could to deny this by wearing boys' clothing, flattening her developing breasts and wearing her hair short in a boyish manner. In spite of her parents' wishes, she continued to act and appear male.

Several years later, I learned that she had contacted clinics in New York City, where surgery was done to alter sexual appearances. She was determined to change her sex via surgical and hormonal treatment.

I was wondering what the saints of the past would think of this phenomenon.

I went around to all the members of the committee to get their opinions. To my surprise, they seemed to be almost completely unaware of the existence of persons who felt that they were not in the right sexual body and thus had sexual identity confusion and conflict.

I advised the group that there was little evidence to show that the issue of sexual identity was a problem determined by psychological growth or poor parenting. Attempts to show that identity issues resulted from physical, hormonal problems have been inconclusive, although further research is being done in this area. So what did the saints think about sexual identity? They hadn't the faintest idea. They, in turn, shook their heads and said that the whole identity problem was a mystery to them.

The discussion among the committee members returned to sexual preferences. It went on for a long time without coming to a firm conclusion. Some members were enlightened to some extent, but no member was persuaded that his or her view was the ultimate truth except St. Paul, who was adamant in condemning homosexuality.

One thought came to me. Since folks with sexual identity issues and preferences for homosexuality were in heaven,

God must have been gracious and included them as well. Heterosexuality did not appear to be a requirement for admission to heaven. On the other hand, perhaps it was not charity at all on God's part, since He created folks who seemed to have little or no choices in sexual preferences. God apparently doesn't condemn or punish those whom He has created.

I thought it was a good discussion, and I thanked the group for coming. I resolved to arrange a time for another summit meeting of this kind at a later date.

Well, I wish I could give you the answers. As for me, I just have to put these questions on the back burner for future consideration. I'm no authority on the ethics of these matters and have no theological degree. I'm just a retired psychiatrist who made the final spiritual leap in a dream to eternity. But these questions still concern me. Maybe after a stay in heaven, these things will be revealed to us. So far, it appears that God is much more inclusive in heaven than we on Earth imagined. If I find out any more on this interesting but enigmatic subject, I will let you know.

Well I'm getting a bit tired of flying from one group to another, and I need a break. You've heard of eternal rest. You thought that consisted of lying around all day doing nothing but watching the clouds and singing. We humans always want to regress to childhood and be taken care of by Big Mama or Big Daddy. But that's not God's way in heaven.

No! God means you to keep busy here and make yourself useful. You know the old saying about the devil finding work for idle hands. Maybe the devil still has some influence here. Anyway, I bet you thought your work on Earth was done once you reached heaven, and now you could simply rest forever. No sir-ree Bob! But here you can do far more in one day than you could in a year of Earth time, and you don't need rest.

Although I had become an ambassador for God, as I told

you, group membership was required for one's stay in heaven. And not being much of a joiner on Earth, I could not help but wonder what God would do if I refused to join a group. I don't know if I dare try that. After all, being thrown out of heaven soon after arriving doesn't sound like a good way to go.

A quote from St. Peter,
**"But the God of all grace... make you
perfect, stablish, strengthen and settle you."**

1 Peter 5:10

CHAPTER 19

After seeing a number of these groups, it again bothered me why most of the inhabitants in heaven were so busy improving themselves. On Earth, I was led to believe that in heaven all would be perfect, and we would be able to take it easy and relax, listening to angels playing their harps and waiting for any heavenly surprises, which God was certainly capable of displaying.

I remembered the talk I had earlier with St. Peter. He was annoyed at my impatience and hinted at the possibility that he would elaborate on just what heaven's frenetic activity is all about.

So I tried to reach him again. I knew he was busy, but he promised me he would enlighten me on the big question I had. But when I approached him, he again appeared grouchy and annoyed. Wow! Even here in heaven a saint can have these earthly feelings. I thought everyone would be joyful and content.

After a considerable delay, St. Peter resigned himself to my persistence and agreed to give me a few minutes, so I plunged directly into the subject.

"You know what I'm puzzled by? Why do the inhabitants of heaven have to be engaged in so much work, and when will it all end?"

It looked like I would finally get an answer.

He gave me a pat on the back and said, "Well, my son, it's a long story, but I will try to make it brief. Over the centuries that humans struggled for survival, life was hard.

"Humans had to endure many trials just to stay alive. They had to fight diseases, unpredictable weather, earthquakes, floods, plagues and the wiles of animal life on Earth. Their children died young; women died in childbirth; plagues caused many to suffer and die at all ages.

"But God gave humankind a desire to live out his earthly life – a resilience to persevere through whatever faced man or woman.

"As the centuries went on, life became easier for many, although much of the world continued to suffer, especially in underdeveloped areas. Humans bravely fought illnesses, hunger and changes in their environment. There is a long history of humankind battling these forces of destruction. And although some improvements have been made on Earth to make life more endurable and pleasant, there is still much distress and suffering.

"Meanwhile, God gave humans this innate desire to improve their lot. On Earth, scientists now say that it has become part of a person's genetic makeup. It's in our DNA – the desire to want to survive and improve matters on Earth. In spite of this strong individual drive, nations continue to fight against each other and wars never seem to cease. Only God can help humans deal with those issues.

"So, my son, when those on Earth die and come to heaven, they retain some earthly ways. They can choose a group or are assigned to groups with which they were familiar on Earth; they attempt to continue working on problems that they faced there. That's why you see everyone so busy. It's such a basic, ingrained tendency to try to work at the tasks familiar to them on Earth. It's hard for folks to immediately change themselves from earthly ways.

"You may have noticed that some of the older prophets and saints don't work so hard. They have come to understand that in heaven, it's not necessary to expend so much energy. You will see them sitting around comfortably, engaged in pleasant conversation and occasionally breaking out in familiar hymns, praises and gratitude for God's heavenly rewards.

"Besides that, God has asked these more mature inhabitants to go around to other groups and advise the members on ways to improve their earthly deficiencies. That's why the newer crop of residents work the hardest. It's difficult to fight the DNA that still resides in your heavenly body, even though everyone has a spiritual self as well. I know that when you first come to heaven, these things are hard to understand."

That last comment was certainly an understatement. It reminded me of St. Luke's story of Mother Mary, after the birth of Jesus and the visits from the shepherds, when Luke comments, "she pondered these things in her heart." There certainly was plenty here to ponder. The mystery of it all was overwhelming.

Well, at least it explained all the activity and the existence of groups in heaven.

Then I asked, "St. Peter, how long will this go on? Will there be a time when the inhabitants of heaven will have reached their goal of spiritual development and have a bit of rest?"

"Yes, that will occur, but only in heavenly time."

St. Pete could not refrain from a heavy sigh. "That's a concept that you obviously haven't understood as of yet. Here, one moment is a thousand years. Time does not have the meaning it had on Earth. Be patient and all will be well, my son."

I had to concede that patience was not my strong suit in

heaven. I thanked St. Peter profusely for the explanation about all the activity in heaven.

I then recalled a comment I read recently by theologian-author Frederick Buechner in his book, *Wishful Thinking, a Seeker's ABC.* In a passage on Purgatory, he reviews the Catholic concept of the afterlife and observes that "even with God on their side people do not attain to what Saint Paul calls 'mature manhood, the measure of the stature of the fullness of Christ' (Eph. 4:13) overnight. At best the job is unlikely to be more than the slimmest fraction done by the time they die."

Then, Buechner quotes an Anglican prayer spoken for a person who died: "Grant that, increasing in knowledge and love of thee, he may go from strength to strength, in the life of perfect service, in thy heavenly kingdom." Buechner further comments, "Increasing in knowledge. From strength to strength. Whichever side of the grave you are talking about, life with God apparently involves growth and growing pains."

At almost the same time as reading Buechner, I read a book by C.S. Lewis called *A Grief Observed.* It describes the mourning period after the death of his wife Joy and his religious doubts, anger at God and subsequently renewed faith.

Lewis says, "Her past anguish. How do I know that all her anguish is past? I never believed before – I thought it immensely improbable – that the faithfulest soul could leap straight into perfection and peace the moment death has rattled in the throat. It would be wishful thinking with a vengeance to take up that belief now. H (Joy) was a splendid thing; a soul straight, bright, and tempered like a sword. But not a perfected saint. A sinful woman married to a sinful man; two of God's patients, not yet cured. I know there are not only tears to be dried but stains to be scoured. The sword will be made even brighter."

These two authors, both of whom have given serious thought to religious questions, are saying that the transition to perfection in heaven will be a gradual process and that somehow the souls in heaven will be purified in God's celestial cauldron and eventually made perfect.

After dealing with that ponderous subject, I decided to get back to what else was happening in heaven.

Next, I wanted to visit with my family – perhaps the most meaningful and joyous meeting of all.

**"Conversing with family and friends in
Heaven is hopefully among the greatest
pleasures God offers."**

Richard Roukema

CHAPTER 20

Going back a bit to the time that I arrived in heaven, I was
invited to heaven's version of an orientation session, not unlike
when you accept a new job on Earth. We newcomers were told
a host of things that are part of the heavenly sphere – things that
do not occur on Earth. Many of the routines and conditions in
heaven were quite foreign to me. Some of the questions I had
were answered at these meetings and some had to be postponed
to another time.

But the one area that I was most curious about had to do
with family and close friends who had passed on before me. I
always wondered how this would play out. Fortunately, I got my
answers quickly.

Jesus was asked by the Sadducees about a woman who was
married many times. They asked who would be her husband in
heaven. Jesus said that there is no marriage in heaven. So I saw
friends greeting and engaging their earthly spouses, but not as
married people. Those who were married more than once met
with their spouses at different times and were quite friendly
with each other. There did not seem to be any of the hostility or

animosity which may have existed in earthly times.

The same was true of brothers and sisters, sons and daughters. It was actually hard to tell if the relationship which existed on Earth had been a healthy, congenial one or whether there had been considerable troubles before.

I saw an acquaintance with whom I had a falling out on Earth. I tried to avoid him; he greeted me with a smile.

"Hey, how are you, doc? It's good to see you. What do you say we get together and talk, maybe even do a little traveling all around God's heaven one day?"

I was frankly alarmed at his friendliness, since we did not leave each other on very comfortable terms on Earth. I began to wonder if this was the healing power of heaven, in which God has a profound effect on those who enter the portals and pass through the proverbial golden gates. I agreed to meet with this friend, but I did not anticipate a happy time together, since my earthly emotions were still playing a familiar role here.

As I walked around, I learned that families could get together as on Earth, but they did not spend all their time with each other. Each family member could travel at will in heaven and be in one group or another. One did not feel constrained to report to a family member, for example about when he or she was planning to leave or return home. There was a freedom of movement that was refreshing. And family members never were concerned about where others went or when they were returning.

Also, traveling was completely safe. One never had to worry about accidents or death. Since humans on Earth spent an enormous amount of time concerned about these two possibilities, it was a remarkable heaven that permitted such freedom from the debilitating and stressful obsession with possible disasters.

There was no need for airplanes, trains or cars. Who needed these earthly conveyances, when all one had to do was wish to be somewhere, and it would happen?

Incidentally, about those heavenly couriers we have heard so much about – the angels – legend has it that they need wings to fly around doing their helpful deeds here on Earth. Not so. The many angels here had no wings, and like humans, they merely had to will to be somewhere and in an instant, they were at their destination.

Family members attended various groups, depending on their interests. There was no need for such close communications as there was on Earth. Since there was no child rearing, no financial needs, housing, clothing or nutritional concerns, there was little reason for family members to constantly be involved with each other. Yet the emotions, the closeness, the affection, the love of family were still present, whenever or not anyone wished it to be.

Here in heaven, I had plenty of family to visit. But by some coincidence one of the first people I ran into was my friend Rich, whom I talked about much earlier.

Rich was in heaven too? How could this be, since he seemed so agnostic about religious matters? I found this to be yet another one of heaven's wonderful mysteries. Later, in an interview I have with God, He explains how unbelievers and doubters reach heaven. For now, let me tell you about Rich.

Rich and I talked about our childhood and the great experiences we had living in our Dutch enclave of Prospect Park. Among the many things we recalled, I thanked him for introducing me to my wonderful wife, Marge. He told me that he was delighted that she had become a congresswoman, although he wished she had been a liberal in her political life. No surprise. Rich had once tried to run for what I remember was an assembly seat in New Jersey. His platform was far too liberal for his voters, and his political career ended abruptly.

Rich recalled many of the friendly chats we had in our early years. I remember his outrage and social conscience when he pointed out that a tube of toothpaste probably cost a few cents to make by the manufacturer and yet sold for a dollar at that time. He railed at the social inequities that existed between the rich and the poor.

We talked about the doubts Rich had about heaven and his fluctuating attempts at faith. In our youth we had gone to a conservative religious retreat together, but I do not recall his reaction to it. I suspect that he had many doubts about the firm, unyielding faith of many participants.

I made the observation that many now here in heaven previously had doubts about the hereafter. Grounded in reality and the mundane problems of our earthly existence, it is hard for many individuals to envision life in the hereafter.

I was very delighted to see Rich here, and we vowed to meet many more times to reminisce about life on Earth.

*****

I was determined to visit with my family next. While still in the Netherlands, before immigrating to the Untied States, my parents had seven children who came to the U.S. as young siblings and later grew to adulthood. I was born seven years later – a bit of a surprise, as my mother was forty-seven years old and my father forty-nine. While bearing children in the later years of a woman's life is more common now, it was not at that time, in the 1920s.

My grandparents, uncles, aunts and cousins all remained in Holland. As a result I never knew any of them, except for two uncles, who came to our home to visit on several occasions. As a busy teenager, I failed to appreciate their visits and regarded them as quaint remnants of my parents' past, hardly important to me. I wish now that I had had long conversations with them about Holland and the relatives living there.

Here in heaven I began my visits. I knew it would take a long time. I started with my dear mother, my five brothers and two sisters. We had a good time talking about some of the pleasant memories of our past days on Earth.

I was especially pleased to express my love and affection to my mother for all her support, devotion and belief in me as I was growing up. She was a quiet, devout, patient person, who rarely complained about anything. While she never seemed to worry about me, I am certain that she prayed about me daily.

I remember well my comment sometime after my father died. I was sixteen years old. My mother had meager savings, and we were hardly secure financially. I said to my mother,

"Well, I guess I won't be able to go to college. We can't afford it."

Without missing a beat, she replied in her low-key quiet manner with an economy of words, "Don't worry." Implied in this was an assurance that somehow, through lots of prayer and hard work, it will happen. My mother proceeded to take in boarders and managed to save money to make it all possible. I worked during the summers as well as twenty hours a week during my school years. It made for a very dull social life, but it enabled me to obtain a college degree.

When I took off on my own, hitch-hiking to college in Arizona, my mother did not hear from me for weeks. We never thought of using the phone; the cost was prohibitive. I relied on post cards to inform her how I was doing and where I was living. I left home in September and did not return until June. Christmas at home? Spring break? Not a chance. That was the year of the song, "I'm Dreaming of a White Christmas." Living in the desert of Arizona at the State College, the song had a special meaning to me.

Although I had thanked my mother for all she had done while still on Earth, it was a joy to do it again. How sweet were the memories.

My siblings had much to do with my early childhood. Only

one of them had a high school and college education. The others finished elementary school and went to work to support the family. They were all much older: the oldest, Andrew, twenty-two years older than me, and the one closest in age, John, nine years older. They were so much more like uncles and aunts than siblings.

I thanked them all for being there for me, especially my brother Bert, who was like a father to me. He took me swimming and skating at local ponds and to the ice rink at the former World's Fair Grounds in New York City, where I could participate in speed skating races on Saturday mornings every winter. He alone made it his mission to help me grow up, in spite of his low income as a baker. At the time, I did not realize that it must have been a financial sacrifice for him and his wife to take me to so many places.

One of Bert's co-workers told me, in later years, that Bert was worried about me as a child and adolescent, and felt he had to help me. For that, I was always very grateful. I had thanked him for helping me get through my early years when we were still on Earth. Here in heaven, I again expressed my gratitude to him.

My brother Peter had a wonderful interest in life, read widely and was a competent amateur painter. While he was still on Earth, we spent many hours over lunch, talking about the past, particularly about our family life. Peter loved to tell stories. He talked about his life in Holland as a child. He remembered seeing a train come by his home filled with Dutch soldiers returning from the front lines after World War I had ended. The troops were so delighted to be back that they ripped the buttons off their uniforms and threw them to the girls standing alongside the railroad tracks.

Peter also told me that there was a small store adjacent to their home in Holland. The proprietor thought nothing of selling cigarettes to children there who were only six or seven years old. Some things have changed.

I talked with my brother Jack, who was an avid hunter – the Nimrod of the family. He took me on his milk route on early summer mornings in my childhood. I enjoyed the thrill of driving the milk truck from one stop to another before I had my driver's license.

I remember one Sunday evening when Jack and I were sitting next to each other in church awaiting the beginning of the worship service (We always went to two church services on Sunday, plus Sunday school.) and he showed me the new ring on his hand, which he had recently purchased. He said that the ring had 14 carats and quickly added, "And I don't know how many beets." As a youngster, I found this comment hilarious, and it made me giggle uncontrollably. This was not exactly proper behavior in our staid Calvinist church. I always enjoyed Jack's sense of humor.

I spent some time with my sister, Grace, whose home I often visited to play with my nephew, Dan, who was three months younger than me.

Next I greeted my sister Marie, with whom I had frequent lunches before she died. She had always been kind to me. Occasionally, before she was married, she took me with her to a lake where she worked as a household domestic for a family. I never dreamed that families had second homes for fishing, boating and swimming. Sweet memories!

I was delighted to see my brother Andrew again. He had the misfortune of being an alcoholic. He was my oldest sibling and lived at home with us. He never married and always appeared to me as a misunderstood man. After several confrontations with the "consistory" at our local Dutch church for his alcoholism and his failure to attend church, he was ceremoniously "excommunicated" from the fold. I was a child when this happened.

A few years later, when I went off to college, I came to have more appreciation for Andrew's predicament. For a class in sociology, I wrote a paper in an attempt to explain the roots of alcoholic behavior. I am certain that this experience of thinking about and dealing with Andrew was one of the forerunners of my interest in psychiatry. I felt that Andrew was more to be pitied than censured. So when I saw him in heaven, I greeted him warmly and expressed my joy about seeing him there. I was glad to see that even if an earthly church had excluded him, the mercy of heaven took him in. Wonderful!

The brother closest to me in age was John. He was nine years older. Our common interest in speed skating was our only shared experience. Before he died at eighty-two of lymphoma, I visited him in Florida. We had some satisfying talks about life and the terminal illness he was facing. It was a good meeting. He seemed prepared to meet his Maker and his faith sustained him. I was glad I had made the effort to visit him.

There were many other relatives in heaven – nephews who had died prematurely and in-laws, too many to mention. But I must talk about one of them – my dear sister-in-law, Aurora. During my adolescence, she lived on the first floor of our two-family house, while we lived on the second floor. Aurora or "Ar" was like another mother to me. She was married to my brother Jack. He and I were the only siblings to marry outside of the Dutch culture. Imagine that! Ar was from an Armenian immigrant family and my wife Marge was of Italian descent.

Ar saw the need to counsel me and listen to my teenage woes about school, peer relationships and anything else I wanted to confide in her. She was wonderfully understanding.

I have an old picture of Ar holding me when I was about two or three years old. Her love for me is obvious in the picture and was always felt throughout her years on earth. After finishing dinner with my mother upstairs in our two-family house, I would often go downstairs to my brother's apartment to finish off their meals. Teenage appetites for food seem to know no limits. I remember a veiled reference to me as "the human garbage pail."

Ar even volunteered in my wife's campaign for U.S. Congress. I was so happy to meet with her again. We embraced for a long time. I thanked her profusely for what she had done. It is hard to imagine what life would have been like without her.

Most folks on Earth have questions and unresolved issues left over after each friend or family member dies. For example, children wonder how a parent felt about them when the parent dies prematurely.

This came as a huge surprise to me, and I was delighted and a bit anxious when I saw my own father. I wondered what he would say. I was sixteen when he died after a brief illness. We never had a close relationship, and I always felt there was much left unsaid. I remembered him being unemotional, not given to expressions of affection or praise.

Unfortunately, he had to work ten to twelve hours at night as a baker. After sleeping a few hours in the morning, he then managed our huge garden and fed the chickens that provided our large family with eggs. As if it were a religious ritual, each Saturday he took one of the hens from the chicken coop and ceremoniously put its head on a block of wood and sacrificed the hen for our Sunday dinner. All this hard labor was necessary in response to the dark days of the economic depression of the 1930s. During that time, my father was unemployed for two years.

I have only two fond memories of my father. One was his appearance on the local Oldham pond on a cold winter day, when he used his antique Dutch ice skates. They consisted of a three-inch-wide wooden platform that was the length of his shoe. Metal blades fitted into a grove on the bottom. Several straps were attached in the front and back of the skates to hold them on to winter boots. That was an unusual sight to see – my father gliding along the ice, upright with his hands behind his back, the only skater with Dutch skates. It was right out of an eighteenth century Dutch painting.

On another occasion, father took me to Paterson on a bus to have my eyeglasses repaired. Upon returning home, we stopped at a drug store which sold ice cream. It was there that he bought me an ice cream cone – the one and only occasion he would do so. Father had little time for a young active kid running around, interested only in sports. I recall irritability and anger from him and a fear of his verbal and physical outbursts. I felt little overt affection from him, although I am certain it was in his heart.

A friend who is older than me recalls seeing my father bringing me to school on my first day of kindergarten. I have no memory of that event. My guess is there were many other times that he did things for me, of which I have no memory. In adult life as time has gone on, I have felt much more empathetic for my father's difficult task in trying to survive with his large family. As a young child, it was difficult to understand this.

Here in heaven, he seemed free of fatigue and had a wonderful relaxed expression on his face. He seemed to be joyful, happy and he greeted me with unusual enthusiasm.

"How are you my boy? It's so good to see you. Welcome to heaven. I have been waiting for you. You have been on my mind for a long time. I have been eager to explain some things to you about what happened on Earth. Let me begin to tell you how things were at that time. When you came into the family, I was almost fifty years old. Your mother and I did not expect another child. It seemed like an additional burden for the family. I felt stressed and overworked.

"Looking back on those events, I want to tell you how sorry I have been for not taking the time to get to know you better on

Earth. I was so busy working every night at the bakery and so tired during the day with other responsibilities, like our large garden and the chickens. I know now I did not take enough time with you. With our big family, there were many responsibilities. It was constant work, work, work, all the time. Once in a while, your mother and I went to a friend's house for company on a Saturday night. But that was so unusual."

I suddenly realized that he had lost his Dutch accent. What? No accents in heaven? At first that struck me as being rather boring. But it did help everyone be understood when they talked. Then I realized again, as I mentioned earlier, that it was not English that heaven's inhabitants were speaking. It was more like an Esperanto.

Father went on. "I guess I hoped your brothers would take care of you. And they did help out a lot. But I was wrong to not take time out for you. A son needs his father. I am proud of how things went for you. I wish I could have been there to see you work your way through college and become a doctor, something that I never dreamed any of my children would do. Then you married Marge, had children and grandchildren, and Marge became a U.S. Congresswoman. How wonderful!

"I want you to know that I mourned with you on the loss of your son, Todd, when he was only seventeen years old. That had to be horrible for you and your family. I have met Todd here in heaven, and he is a fine young man. I am sure you are proud of him."

We embraced for a long time. I told my father that I loved him, and that I was also sorry that I did not make more of an effort to express my feelings on Earth. As we talked, he told me about many of the things that happened in Holland before he came to America – things that I have long wondered about.

"Those were difficult times after World War I. I felt responsible for my large family of seven children in Holland. I couldn't find work, and I needed to start another life. We had to stand in bread lines just to get some food. I knew I had to do something quickly for my family. That's when I came to America with your oldest brother, Andrew, much against my family's wishes. Things were hard that first year. Instead of working during the daytime as a baker, like I did in Holland, I had to work nights, which as you know lasted for the rest of my life. No one had told me that this is the way they did things in America.

"I had some second thoughts about whether I had made the right decision about coming to America, but a couple of good friends convinced me to stay. That's when I borrowed some money and sent for the rest of the family. Of course, you had not yet been born. You know, it was seven years later when you arrived. I had great doubts about how I was going to support such a big family of eight, but by then some of your brothers were already working. That helped to keep us going from day to day. Then when World War II broke out, I was really glad we had moved to America. You were in high school, and everyone in the family had jobs. In those days that was how you measured success.

"Meanwhile in Holland, the situation was bad for the family. They were short on food and clothing and lived through difficult times. I remember sending clothes and money to those in Holland. However, none of the family there suffered under the German occupation, like they did in other parts of Holland.

"I was very proud of you at that time, but I'm afraid I never told you. We Dutch were never people who bragged about ourselves or complimented each other. We never expressed ourselves the way people do now. I don't ever remember my own mother or father in Holland saying they loved me. That's just the way we were, even though we felt loved. When we left to come to America, my father said I was doing the wrong thing, but he never made any fuss about it or showed any emotion.

Well, that was a long time ago.

"Since being here in heaven, I have been able to see my own parents and revisit the past and express to them my thanks for all they did for me when I was still in Holland. It's wonderful to do that. And it's so good to see you. All your brothers and sisters are here too, as is your dear mother. I am now close to them as never before."

I was overcome with joy. This is what I missed on Earth – intimacy and a close relationship with my father. At last! This is really heaven!

"It's so good to see you and talk about things that I always wondered about and never thought to ask you. We have to meet again and talk some more," I said. We lingered a while longer and vowed to continue our meetings often.

I then looked around for our son Todd, who died of leukemia a few days after his seventeenth birthday. His interests were so much like mine; it was striking. In addition to his love of football and skiing, he was a reader, and had a keen interest in psychology. He expressed a desire to become a physician, and it would not have surprised me if he had chosen psychiatry as a field in which to work. But none of that would come about. Instead, he went through a two-year illness, during which he was quite active until a short time before the end. He had a recurrence of acute leukemia, and within a week he died.

As a father, I felt that I had not done enough for him on Earth. I did not reach out emotionally to him and express my love in an overt way. Yes, I and other family members did do a great number of things for him and expressed our love by our acts, but not in words. I wished I could have told him that he was going to live through it all. I did not have the heart to tell him or the rest of the family of the poor prognosis that his doctor had given me. I felt too protective of them all, and thereby did them a great disservice. Neither I nor anyone in the family was able to tell Todd that we would miss him or how we loved him. We missed opportunities to say our goodbyes.

Looking back on this horrendous experience and loss, we were all in denial of the reality of his impending death. If I did not accept the fact that he would die, how could I talk to him about my love for him, and how I would miss him? How could I speak to him of heaven, if I did not expect him to die? I do not know the answer to what we could have done to make him feel better or acknowledge what he was going through. Even now after thirty-four years, I feel we could have done something, but even as a psychiatrist, words fail me in knowing what that would have been.

Here in heaven, I would have the opportunity to reunite with Todd and tell him how much we loved him and how sorry we have been for not meeting his needs better than we did.

Can you imagine the first meeting after all those years? When I saw Todd he looked as robust as ever. He greeted me with open arms, and we hugged for a long time. Heavenly tears flowed in abundance. The joy of meeting him was not like any earthly encounter. It had a special celestial, emotive, spiritual blend that one could only have in heaven. Todd looked so relaxed, content and happy.

"Todd, you don't know how wonderful it is to see you." He immediately assured me that he thought of the family often and was always interested in what we were doing. He was especially proud of what his mother had done in her career as a congresswoman. We talked extensively about his brother Greg and his sister Meg and their families. He would so have enjoyed them, had he remained on Earth. I know he would have been a great uncle and a marvelous father and husband.

After a long time reviewing earthly matters, I made an attempt to ask Todd about our relationship while he was undergoing his illness. When I first asked him about it, he seemed a bit puzzled.

"I'm not sure what you mean that you could have done a better job of helping me. You gave blood a number of times, took me to the doctor, brought me to Vermont on vacations and even skiing at Vail that one winter. I had a good time with all that. And the motorbike in Vermont was a big thrill for me, Dad!"

"Yes, I know you enjoyed those things, and we were happy to do them for you, but I'm talking about more emotional expressions of how we felt about you and what might happen to you."

Todd shook his head. "I don't know what you mean, Dad. How could you have talked to me about heaven if you really felt I would continue to live on Earth? It was hard for me to cope with the illness, but I realized it was hard on you too. I could see it in your faces, a mixture of hope and resignation. I could see the sadness, especially in mother's eyes. It was a very difficult time. I would like to speak with mother about this too. I hope she is resigned to it by this time. Certainly, here in heaven, we will all understand things better."

I appreciated what Todd had to say, but I still felt that more conversations were necessary before I would feel right about my relationship with him. Somehow, I still felt there was more I could have done on Earth. But what that could have been, I could not imagine. I vowed to return to this emotional area soon.

Even through the tears, it was a joyful reunion – one I had long anticipated, although I was not certain how it would turn out. But heaven's joys are wonders of which we have trouble conceiving. We are too accustomed to earthly ways. But God does not disappoint His sheep. In heaven, He has the best surprises!

Other family relationships are also healed in heaven. Husbands and wives often are left with unanswered issues between them, especially when death occurs suddenly. Also, folks wonder about how deceased friends felt about them after dying. All such questions left over from earthly relationships are answered in heaven, but not all at once. At any given time, relatives could be contacted to inquire about earthly feelings and reactions. As you might expect, if the contact between two individuals ended on Earth in a disastrous manner or even on a bitter note, these unfinished issues could be resolved. God provided a way in heaven for restoration, forgiveness and redemption. Of all the wonderful gifts that God makes available in heaven, this is among the most valuable reward to disturbed souls.

Another question. How old will I be in heaven? St. Augustine wrote in *The City of God* that everyone would be at the prime of their earthly life, which he estimated would be around age thirty. But I discovered you can choose to be any age for as long as you wish. For example, if you wanted to re-experience childhood or adolescence you could do so for as long as it pleased you. If you died as a child, you could become an adult in heaven if you desired. Changes could be made to any age just by wishing it were so.

As it turned out, I was surprised at the variety of things one could do in heaven and how different it was from Earth. Some complained of boredom, but folks always had something to occupy themselves. Those folks on Earth who were constantly trying to improve themselves found that heaven suited their basic view of change and growth, while those who never looked toward a better self found it harder to get along and be content in heaven.

"Jesus does not think dogmatically. He formulates no doctrine. He is far from judging any man's belief by reference to any standard of dogmatic correctness. Nowhere does he demand that his hearers sacrifice thinking to believing."

Albert Schweitzer, *Out of My Life and Thought*

CHAPTER 21

After a heavenly pause for rest, which here is almost instantaneous, I got to thinking about another group that could possibly be here. It was not a certainty, however, that God would grant them a place in heaven. I remembered a number of friends that I had on Earth who were either agnostics or atheists. They had all been exposed in one way or another to the Bible and to other religions. They knew about the accepted biblical way to heaven through faith in God and his plan for salvation.

Yet these folks, many of whom were outstanding citizens in their communities, never acknowledged the existence of God or signed on to any formal religious faith or institution. These were not among the vast numbers who had never heard of any gospel of Jesus that preached the way to heaven. They had all been exposed to traditional Western religions.

The people I am thinking about are your friends and my friends, like my childhood buddy, Rich, who I told you about at the beginning and in the last chapter. He had a great deal of exposure to religion, but appeared to be agnostic at the end. Those like Rich had heard about the religions of the world, but had great doubts or rejected them as being irrelevant and untrue.

What was God's plan for this tremendous group, many of whom led exemplary moral lives?

It was often observed on Earth that people who are agnostics or atheists often lived lives that were more in keeping with the morality of various religions than some of the members of religious faiths. I need mention only the TV evangelists, who became wealthy preaching the gospel, only to confess to outrageous behaviors done in secret. How was God going to resolve this irony?

I could see that the answer to this question would require a committee or perhaps a direct answer from God Himself. I thought about who I might ask to join such a group. The members of my last committee came immediately to mind. But there was a problem with each of them. The Old Testament prophets had no exposure to God's plan of salvation as revealed in the New Testament. Even Solomon, with all his great wisdom, could not make any relevant comments on this issue.

The New Testament saints, including St. Paul, were very clear on salvation and the route to eternal life. They are quite explicit on the need for belief in Christ as the Savior and the reconciliation to God through faith. The early Christian saints such as St. Augustine, and later St. Thomas, were equally certain on the plan of salvation, and to my knowledge, they did not view agnostics and atheists as among the saved; these unbelievers were destined to the fires of hell.

Other theologians such as Luther and Calvin had their view of the elect and predestination, which included relatively few humans and certainly left no room for any doubting Thomases and atheists. Heaven would be sparsely populated, and hell would be overrun by a huge population of sinners and many of

God's creatures who had never heard of the gospel.

As is well known, Blaise Pascal, the seventeenth century mathematician, physician and religious philosopher, wrote about an interesting wager in his noted book *Penses*.

Rather than give in to his doubts, Pascal made the intellectual bet that the plan of salvation was true, thus eliminating the possibility that he would be on the wrong side. He contended that it would be better to believe in Christianity than risk losing the reward of heaven by continual doubt or outright rejection of the faith.

The Catholic Popes have for the most part been clear on their theology, leaving little doubt as to who would reach heaven – after a period of time in purgatory – and who would spend the rest of eternity in hell.

I thought of the modern theologians like Barth, Kirkegaard, Tillich and others, but I despaired of getting a sound answer from them regarding the question of what happens to those who remain agnostic or atheist. I felt like I needed to hear directly from God. Perhaps He would give some hint of the outcome for these humans.

So I tried to get another audience with God. You will remember that the last time I attempted this, it was not easy. But since I was working as God's ambassador, I thought that I might have an in with God; perhaps getting his celestial ear would be far less difficult this time around. You will recall that I asked God about this group of non-believers the last time I talked directly with Him.

Well, it took a while, since God was rather busy. But I needed more clarity. Although He is omnipotent, He has no need to conform to time as we know it. In the biblical age, He did speak and act in accordance with time, so that His followers would understand Him.

Similarly, here in heaven, He allowed for time to pass so as not to confuse the inhabitants.

In spite of His attending to the many galaxies and planets in the Universe, God finally, through my contact with St. Peter, granted me an audience. Again, I could not describe Him well, since He was constantly changing. But whatever His form was at any given time, I could hear His voice quite well coming through the mist and clouds. The resonance of His voice thrilled me when He asked,

"What is it my son, what are you concerned about now?"

I began with some apprehension, as I was not confident that God would appreciate my asking Him about those folks on Earth who did not accept Him or even believe that He existed. But then I remembered that He was gracious and would probably understand my questioning ways. I approached the issue this way.

"Almighty God, we humans do have a lot of questions. You know it is part of how you created us. I have asked many things since being here in heaven. But one thing troubles me greatly. I had many friends on Earth who did not accept the fact of Your existence. Yet they were people of high moral standards. I know that You have regarded everyone that existed as basically sinful and therefore in need of forgiveness and redemption. I believe that it was the prophet Isaiah who said that even our best works "are as filthy rags." But what of those who have not recognized sin or the need for cleansing? What about those who saw no hope or need of Heaven?"

I heard thunder, loud unremitting thunder. Did I disturb God? Or was He just warming up to give me a piece of His eternal mind? I trembled at first, but then He came through with the calm of heaven in a voice that was musical and sweet. I was suddenly relaxed as though I had received a heavenly massage throughout my entire heavenly body.

God began in a low key, soft voice,

"My son, you do have a way of asking the big questions. It points to your giving much thought to your existential journey, which I have not made easy for you humans. I deliberately made it puzzling, so that you would give deep thought to My existence and the meaning of your life.

"Although you have asked me this question before, I realize that it must be very troubling to you to bring it up again. Let me begin by saying that humans are imperfect beings. A slight change in your physical makeup makes all the difference in how you behave and how you are able to function. For example, a minor alteration in your body chemistry can make all the difference in your mood, causing severe depression or other mental illness. An injury to your brain can make you behave in ways that are not characteristic of your former self. A loss of memory changes personality as well as behavior in drastic ways.

"Hereditary factors can alter the course of your life with diseases that you could not have imagined. Slight changes in your genetic structure can cause behaviors that are unusual, some even harmful to other humans. Traumatic events can alter your life and make you fearful and act in uncharacteristic ways. And, of course, the culture to which you are born can have a huge influence on how you behave. Your early life can be influenced for good or ill depending upon what happens to you.

"In many ways you are like a reed in the wind, a tree buffeted about with the storms of life. Sometimes you weather the storms well; at other times you are uprooted and sometimes even destroyed by those around you who have malevolent intent.

"Your scientists on Earth are constantly studying the human mind and soul. Each time they discover a new aspect of the human behavior, there are many more questions. The end point of behavior is a combination of hereditary factors, social and physical environment, parenting, education and many more things. Add to this a degree of free will that I have given to humans, and you can see that it is very difficult to figure out why anyone commits a given act, be it the gift of altruism or the horror of crimes such as serial murder.

"So you see, I have not made it easy for humans to understand behavior or even believe in Me, their Creator. It makes the journey very hard for some and less so for others. Those that have been blessed with physical comforts and a good living environment are often quick to blame the actions of those who are deprived of such luxuries. This is an unfortunate tendency of human nature – one that needs perfecting.

"Humankind has been quick to judge the actions of others. My Son, Jesus, spoke to this issue on a number of occasions, as when He said, 'Judge not that ye be not judged.' But no human does this perfectly.

"And no human is in a position to say who will be in heaven and who will be excluded. While humans are on Earth, I want them to try to live the best lives they are capable of living. However, I am aware that many will fall short of living a moral life, of helping their neighbors, giving to the poor and helping those in need, whether in local communities or in other countries. Many will be willfully evil and commit horrendous crimes. But all are human and all are My creatures.

"Let me ask you, son. If you were the Creator of the universe with many planets, all with humans on them, would you want to see any of your creatures perish? Or would you want to see them all living after their earthly life, with a soul that is able to work toward perfection here in heaven?

"You have traveled all over heaven and have seen the various groups. All have fallen short of perfection. All need a lot of work to help them toward the search for a degree of perfection. I have enlisted the prophets and saints to help the others in that path to a more perfect life.

"So it is My will that all should be saved. This is the meaning of the parable of the lost sheep as told by my son, Jesus. I want the one sheep that is lost to be found and come into my heavenly fold. If you were the Creator, wouldn't you want to have all your sheep back in the fold – here in heaven? I know the answer before you can tell me. That is My will and at the end of civilization as you know it – all will eventually come to a perfect heaven.

"Likewise, in the parable of the prodigal son, Jesus made it clear that the father was not concerned about those in the family who had remained at home, but he longed to see the son who had been absent for many years. When he returned, the father rejoiced and prepared a large feast for him. That is a picture of how I feel when any one of My creatures comes to heaven. I want all my children with me on the last day.

"So, my son, it is My will that all should be saved. I know that there are those folks on Earth who think that they have an exclusive right to heaven. But they have an arrogance born of fear and judgment that is unfortunate. My saints and prophets will deal with this problem in heaven. This group of elitists will come to see that they are no better than anyone else, and that it is My will that all will come to perfection, not a small select group.

"Yes, I have determined this outcome from the beginning of the Universe. It has been My intent that all should come to perfection here in heaven."

With that illuminating statement, I felt a cozy, all-engulfing blanket surrounding me, like a heavenly comforter – an earthly reminder, a memory, not unlike what I fondly recall from childhood, after being tucked into my warm bed by my loving mother.

It was an overwhelming experience to have an audience with God. No earthly event can compare; no emotional reaction can describe the insight, the bliss, and comfort of hearing the Word directly from the Creator. It all seemed too good to be true.

The Awakening to Earth.

CHAPTER 22

After this unbelievable experience of talking directly with God about the problem that had so preoccupied me, I suddenly woke up alarmed. Where was I? I looked around and it all appeared familiar – the room, the furnishings, the mirror. I was at home and not in heaven. What had happened? Was it a dream? I know I was in heaven. It was nothing like I had imagined or read about. It was too much to even tell my family about. How could I ever relate what I went through in that dream?

Here I am, still having to wrestle with existential problems. Still an earthling! What do I do now? Try to record what happened in the dream? Why do that? Something had changed within me. It took some time for me to realize the extent of the change that had occurred within my feelings. Was it tranquility, profound relaxation, awe, a celestial spiritual high note? Would it last?

How could a dream have such an effect? Was any of what I had heard in the dream real? Could I rely on what I had learned? Did I really communicate with the prophets, the saints, my family and friends? Did God really talk to me? Is God as forgiving as He had said in the dream? Is He inclusive and wanting all to come to Him? Will all be saved? Jesus is quoted by St. John saying, "And if any man hear my words, and believe not, I judge him not: for I came not to judge the world, but to save the world"

(John 12:47).

And finally, in the Acts of the Apostles, St. Peter says, in chapter 10:34, "I perceive that God is no respecter of persons: But in every nation he that feareth him and worketh righteousness is accepted with him."

Is that the final word?

Of course, I do not have the answer. But the thought that all will be saved gives a certain comfort to the idea that I will see my family and friends, my boyhood friend Rich and many others who have enriched my life in a myriad of ways.

God the Creator did not give us the answer to every problem here on Earth. This makes it an enigma as well as interesting. If we knew the answer to everything, our lives would be rather dull. I am reminded of Isaiah 55:8,

"For my thoughts are not your thoughts. Neither are your ways my ways." saith the Lord.

*****

A few years ago, I had lunch with three people, all of whom had been involved for many years as teachers and administrators in a conservative, fundamentalist Bible college. One of those present was a dear friend named Jim, who was a psychologist and a colleague of mine. He had worked with the others in his early years. We had a wonderful discussion about a variety of issues involving cultures, politics, education and religion. It became apparent in our talking that all of those present had undergone changes in their faith perspective since earlier times. They seemed more questioning about the mysteries of the faith, and did not have the absolutist views of their more conservative friends.

One of the three persons at lunch that day ended our conversation by reciting a simple prayer in summary. It was a fitting conclusion to what we had been discussing. I do not know if the prayer is original. But to me, it is a classic! It refers to those – whom we all have met – who speak as though they know with absolute certainty God's plan for us, as though they alone are privy to all the existential problems we face, including all knowledge of heaven, and who will be present there. The prayer goes like this:

"Lord, lead me in the paths of the seekers of truth, but preserve me from those who have already found it."

Along with this insightful prayer, I like to add, "Lord, help me be an eternal seeker, forever discovering more of Your truth."

The dream of my trip to heaven was very enlightening. It opened up many avenues for reflection. I trust that you will join me in imagining this wonderful mystery, which we will see more clearly one day, when the time comes for each of us to pass on to the next world – to heaven.

WALKING ALL OVER GOD'S HEAVEN
QUESTIONS FOR DISCUSSION

Chapters

1. What is your picture of heaven?
   What will residents there do with all their time?
2. What will happen to your good friends who
   are agnostics?
   Will you see them in heaven too?
3. Is it possible that the saints and prophets will be
   there to counsel newcomers?
4. Which of the biblical characters would you most
   like to meet and why?
5. Why do humans form groups that have extreme views
   and are often hostile to others who do not share
   these views?
   Which of the ISMS do you think is the most dangerous?
6. Are there prophets living today? If so, how do we know
   they are valid and speak the truth?
7. Have you ever imagined talking directly to Jesus?
   What would you like to say to Him and ask of Him?
8. Who were your favorite teachers? What did they
   contribute to your emotional and mental growth?
9. Can you imagine political parties in heaven?
   What would they do?
10. Is it possible that Judas would also be in heaven with
    the other disciples?

How forgiving is God?

Can you imagine God creating hell for the eternal punishment of sinners?

11.   How do you rank on the humility scale? How can one be proud of accomplishments and humble at the same time?

12.   What are the worst and best qualities in your doctors?

13.   Are there adventures that you would still like to take? Why are you not taking new risks and seeking fresh dreams?

14.   Are there any historical rulers, potentates, world leaders that you admire?

15.   Have you ever had an epiphany—a sudden revelation that had not occurred to you before?

Can you describe it?

16.   Could you stand living with saints?

Do you know people who are just too good for you to feel comfortable around?

17.   What are the worst and best qualities in your lawyers?

18.   Have you ever thought of what God will do with those whose sexual identities and preferences are different from yours?

Do you think that sexual predators will ever make it to heaven?

19.   What do you think of St. Peter's explanation of human nature?

Will we still have some of our own nature when in heaven?

20.   Do you expect to see your family in heaven?

Who are you most eager to see again?

Will families be together in heaven?

21.   Can you imagine having a conversation with God? What would you most like to ask Him?

Do you think it possible that God would forgive every one and have all His creatures come to heaven regardless of their earthly behaviors?

22. Are you tolerant of those who declare they possess absolute truth?

Do you find life on earth and existence in the after-life too complex to understand?

Why?

ABOUT THE AUTHOR

Richard Roukema, M.D.,F.A.P.A. is Clinical Associate Professor of Psychiatry at the University of Medicine and Dentistry of New Jersey. He received his residency training at the Psychiatric Institute, Columbia University College of Physicians and Surgeons, and Rockland State Hospital.

Dr. Roukema is the former Clinical Director of Mental Health and Medical Staff President at the Christian Health Care Center in Wyckoff, New Jersey. He was in private practice for many years. In his position at the University, he published books and journal articles and won awards for teaching medical students and residents. Dr. Roukema received the 1994 "Psychiatrist of the year" award from the National Alliance for the Mentally Ill and the "TOP Docs" award in New Jersey in 1998. He is married to the former U.S. Congresswoman Marge Roukema and has two children and five grandchildren.

Dr. Roukema is author of *Counseling for the Soul in Distress, What Every Religious Counselor Should Know About Emotional and Mental Illness* (Haworth Pastoral Press, 2003) and a book for the general reader called *What Every Patient, Friend, Family and Caregiver Needs to Know About Psychiatry* (American Psychiatric Pub. Inc., 2003). He is also the author of *Spouse of the House,* a book about the elections and tenure of Marge Roukema to the U.S. Congress, and *Shepherding the Shepherd, Negotiating the Stress of Ministry, a mental health guide for clergy.*

**Intermedia
Publishing Group**

Do you need a speaker?

Do you want Richard Roukma to speak to your group or event? Then contact Larry Davis at: **(623) 337-8710** or email: **ldavis@intermediapr.com** or use the contact form at: **www.intermediapr.com**.

Whether you want to purchase bulk copies of *Walking All Over God's Heaven* or buy another book for a friend, get it now at: **www.imprbooks.com**.

If you have a book that you would like to publish, contact Terry Whalin, Publisher, at Intermedia Publishing Group, (623) 337-8710 or email: twhalin@intermediapub. com or use the contact form at: www.intermediapub.com.